Teamwork Test Prep

READING AND MATH

GRADE

6

by Drew Johnson and
Cynthia Johnson

Illustrations by Marty Bucella

Carson-Dellosa Publishing Company, Inc.
Greensboro, North Carolina

Credits

Authors: Drew Johnson and Cynthia Johnson
Editors: Kelly Morris Huxmann, Sabena Maiden, and Donna Walkush
Layout Design: Mark Conrad
Production: River Road Graphics
Inside Illustrations: Marty Bucella
Cover Design: Annette Hollister-Papp

ISBN: 0-88724-272-3

 **Table of Contents**

 **Introduction**

Across the country, thousands of students and teachers spend countless hours preparing for state standardized tests. This focus on repetitive, high-intensity preparation can increase student anxiety, cause "burnout," and lead students to develop strong negative feelings about testing—all undesirable effects that can ultimately hurt students' test performance.

Teamwork Test Prep offers a change of pace. This book provides fun, creative group activities that sharpen students' test-taking abilities, build their confidence, instill positive attitudes toward the tests they are facing, and provide them with a supportive network of classmates who share their goals.

Teamwork Test Prep is an effective alternative to the drills and drudgery often associated with the process of getting students ready for standardized tests. It provides everything you need to transform test preparation from a necessary chore into a group experience that is rewarding in its own right. Here is what you will find inside this book:

✗ A short history of the rise of state testing programs

✗ A list of resources where you can find more information about your state's tests and learning standards

✗ An explanation of our unique "teamwork" approach to test preparation and your key role as "coach"

✗ Short, reproducible diagnostic tests to measure your students' current abilities and gauge their progress

✗ Important test-taking skills and strategies that students can really use

✗ Engaging group activities specifically designed to hone important reading and math skills

✗ Practice tests that help students prepare for the real thing

Use *Teamwork Test Prep* as a self-contained test preparation program, or supplement your existing program with the activities and diagnostics in this book. Either approach is sure to give your students a boost—in their scores, spirits, and confidence!

Understanding Your State's Tests

Understanding the issues involved with state assessment tests is the first step in preparing your students for success. Although standards may vary from state to state, there are many important issues that are common to all states when it comes to standardized testing. The practical information found in this chapter can be used by teachers anywhere in the United States. It includes:

✗ The basic components of the No Child Left Behind Act
✗ An overview of the test development process at the state level
✗ A checklist of questions to help you familiarize yourself with your state's tests
✗ Valuable resources you can use to gather more information about your state's tests

The No Child Left Behind Act

Passed in January 2002, the No Child Left Behind Act (NCLB) represents the federal government's most recent plan for education reform. The centerpiece of the law mandates annual testing in reading and math, beginning in 2005, for all public school students in grades three through eight. Although this is a federal mandate, the government has not established a concurrent set of national standards that all states must follow. Instead, states have the flexibility to create its own "statewide accountability systems." Within these systems, each state typically:

✗ Sets academic standards in each content area for what students should learn and master at each grade level
✗ Develops tests that are aligned with the standards
✗ Uses those tests to collect objective data to analyze how students are doing (and often to show how various socioeconomic subsets are faring in the educational system)
✗ Makes improvements in curriculum, instruction, and assessment based on test results

Whatever systems the state chooses to develop and follow, it is ultimately held responsible for the performance of its students. Students must perform at a proficient level—according to each state's standards—within 12 years of NCLB's enactment. Each state must also share its data or test results with local communities in the form of reports. These reports are designed to inform parents and other stakeholders of how student learning is measuring up to the state's standards and educational goals. Consequences of the testing results may differ from state to state. In one state, a low-performing district that shows no improvement might have its superintendent replaced, while in another, a school with continued "failing" grades might find itself taken over by the state education agency.

Since many states already have some form of state testing in place, the passage of No Child Left Behind has not drastically changed current testing patterns. Tests are being revamped, however, to meet NCLB requirements. Since each state has flexibility in setting its own standards, the tests students will take are likely to reflect what they already know or are currently learning. For example, a standardized reading test established for sixth graders in Iowa would be relevant for students in that state, but not necessarily for sixth graders in California.

How State Assessment Tests Are Developed

The first step in developing state assessment tests is to establish learning standards. This helps ensure equal learning opportunities for all students and, thus, equal opportunities for academic achievement. Standards are usually divided by grade level and content area or discipline, and some are further divided by course number or subdiscipline. These standards form the basis of the scope and sequence of skills assessed, and, in some cases, delineate actual content covered, as in social studies or science.

Standards developed in each state set the tone for instruction and achievement. Most state standards reflect carefully derived expectations of what students should know and be able to do at a specific grade level. These expectations of proficiency also establish curriculum frameworks. Educators use these standards as a scaffolding to determine the skills, content, and processes that students should learn.

After the standards are established, the actual test development process begins. Although the process varies from state to state, test development generally goes through several stages. Each state's department of education or state educational agency has a specific internal department or division dedicated to curriculum development and assessment. This group of professional educators first evaluates any previous state assessments to see how well they measure current or newly adopted standards. Then, through analysis of similar or previously administered exams and current assessment research, these educators develop testing blueprints to best represent the core standards and essential elements of the curriculum.

The next stage for most states involves developing field tests based on these blueprints. Field tests are written and administered to try out items that may be used later on actual tests. After the field tests have been administered, review committees evaluate the results to determine the appropriateness, accuracy, and alignment of test items.

Benchmark tests may also be developed to set the scoring goals for new assessments or standards. Like field tests, benchmark tests are scored and recorded, but they are not used for accountability purposes at the district, school, or student level. These tests are used to see how well students will perform on the final tests and to help guide instruction.

The actual writing of the tests can vary depending on the state. Some states develop the tests completely within their own education departments. Assessment specialists review and revise test items, which are written by professional item writers hired independently by the education department. Some states, such as Texas and New York, hire former or current teachers to develop test items based on blueprints created by their education departments.

In other states, the tests are outsourced and written by professional educational testing companies that have contracted with the state. Test items are written by company-hired professional writers or, in some cases, by professional writers collaborating with education department staff. These writers use the previously developed test blueprints as guidelines for writing. Each item is written to measure specific content standards and then reviewed by the state's education department for alignment and accuracy.

Once benchmark tests have been developed and administered to students, a passing standard is established based on the results. This passing standard is used to compare how well students should perform versus how well they actually do perform on the real tests.

Finally, the real tests are developed and administered to students. If students do not perform at or above the passing standard, schools use the results to examine factors that may help improve students' scores and, along with them, academic achievement.

Checklist: What You Need to Know about Your State's Tests

Having the information you need about your own state's tests is crucial to your students' achievement. Luckily, this information is readily available. Use the following checklist of questions as a guide in learning about your state's standards and assessment tests:

- ☐ What are the learning standards for each major content area per grade level?
- ☐ What are the most current forms of assessment tests administered at each grade level?
- ☐ What is the state's time frame for developing and administering new assessment tests?
- ☐ What is the schedule of testing dates for each grade level?
- ☐ How are the standards assessed per test, per grade level?
- ☐ What scoring and rating systems are used for the tests?
- ☐ How and when are testing "report cards" disseminated?
- ☐ Is there any additional pre- and post-testing data available?
- ☐ What test preparation materials are available? (test samples, instructional materials, benchmark or other practice tests, etc.)
- ☐ What training is available at the school, district, state, and regional levels for teachers and parents?
- ☐ What are the implications and consequences of the test results for students, teachers, schools, and districts?
- ☐ Who composes the tests and what input may you have on their design?
- ☐ What local, state, regional, and national resources are available that address standardized testing? (organizations, educational boards and agencies, advocacy and research groups, professional and community listservs, Web-based bulletin boards, etc.)
- ☐ Who can you contact at the school or district level for more information? (school dean of instruction, instructional specialist, department chairperson, other administrators, etc.)

The Information You Need: Resources for State Standards and Assessment

Much of the information for the checklist on page 7 is available from the following resources:

National Resources

No Child Left Behind Act Web site
http://www.ed.gov/nclb/landing.jhtml
> This Web site includes separate sections for students, parents, teachers, and administrators. It addresses testing, accountability, reading issues, teachers' roles, and much more. The site also provides links to an E-mail based subscription newsletter, details on policy and legislation, fact sheets, statistics and graphs, state testing information, and additional resources.

United States Department of Education
http://www.ed.gov/index.jhtml
> This site contains information for students, parents, teachers, and administrators on educational priorities, research and statistics, PreK–12 issues, as well as links to other educational resources.

National Education Association
http://www.nea.org/
> The NEA's site includes information on accountability and testing, help for parents, a legislative action center link, various publications, and current educational news.

Education News
http://www.educationnews.org/
> This Web site offers free, education-related information from all states, complete with daily headline stories and a searchable archive.

Teachvision.com
http://www.teachervision.fen.com/lesson-plans/lesson-10279.html
> This site provides an extensive list of resources on No Child Left Behind.

State Education Departments/Agencies

An asterisk (*) denotes a special Web site outlining standards/assessments if available.

Alabama Department of Education
50 North Ripley Street
P.O. Box 302101
Montgomery, AL 36104
Phone: (334) 242-9700
http://www.alsde.edu/html/home.asp

Alaska Department of Education and
Early Development
801 West Tenth Street, Suite 200
Juneau, AK 99801-1878
Phone: (907) 465-2800
Fax: (907) 465-3452
http://www.educ.state.ak.us/home.html
* *http://www.educ.state.ak.us/standards/*
* *http://www.educ.state.ak.us/tls/assessment/*

Arizona Department of Education
1535 West Jefferson Street
Phoenix, AZ 85007
Phone: (602) 542-5393 or (800) 352-4558
http://www.ade.state.az.us/
* *http://www.ade.state.az.us/standards/*

Arkansas Department of Education
#4 Capitol Mall
Little Rock, AR 72201
Phone: (501) 682-4475
http://arkedu.state.ar.us/
* *http://arkedu.state.ar.us/actaap/index.htm*

California Department of Education
1430 N Street
Sacramento, CA 95814
Phone: (916) 319-0800
http://goldmine.cde.ca.gov/
* *http://goldmine.cde.ca.gov/statetests/*

Colorado Department of Education
201 East Colfax Avenue
Denver, CO 80203-1799
Phone: (303) 866-6600
Fax: (303) 830-0793
http://www.cde.state.co.us/index_home.htm
* *http://www.cde.state.co.us/index_stnd.htm*

Connecticut State Department of Education
165 Capitol Avenue
Hartford, CT 06145
Phone: (860) 713-6548
http://www.state.ct.us/sde/

Delaware Department of Education
401 Federal Street
P.O. Box 1402
Dover, DE 19903-1402
Phone: (302) 739-4601
Fax: (302) 739-4654
http://www.doe.state.de.us/index.htm
* *http://www.doe.state.de.us/AAB/*

Florida Department of Education
Office of the Commissioner
Turlington Building, Suite 1514
325 West Gaines Street
Tallahassee, FL 32399
Phone: (850) 245-0505
Fax: (850) 245-9667
http://www.fldoe.org/
* *http://www.firn.edu/doe/curric/prek12/*
   frame2.htm

Georgia Department of Education
2054 Twin Towers East
Atlanta, GA 30334
Phone: (404) 656-2800 or (800) 311-3627
Fax: (404) 651-6867
http://www.doe.k12.ga.us/index.asp
* Georgia Learning Connections Web site:
   http://www.glc.k12.ga.us/
   GLC Phone: (404) 651-5664
   GLC Fax: (404) 657-5183

Hawaii Department of Education
1390 Miller Street
P.O. Box 2360
Honolulu, HI 96804
Phone: (808) 586-3230
Fax: (808) 586-3234
http://doe.k12.hi.us/
* *http://doe.k12.hi.us/standards/index.htm*

Idaho Department of Education
650 West State Street
P.O. Box 83720
Boise, ID 83720-0027
Phone: (208) 332-6800
http://www.sde.state.id.us/Dept/
* *http://www.sde.state.id.us/admin/standards/*

Illinois State Board of Education
100 North First Street
Springfield, IL 62777-0001
Phone: (217) 782-4321 or (866) 262-6663
Fax: (217) 524-4928
TTY: (217) 782-1900
http://www.isbe.state.il.us/
* *http://www.isbe.state.il.us/ils/*

Indiana Department of Education
Room 229, State House
Indianapolis, IN 46204-2798
Phone: (317) 232-6610
Fax: (317) 232-8004
http://doe.state.in.us/welcome.html
* *http://doe.state.in.us/asap/welcome.html*

Iowa Department of Education
Grimes State Office Building
Des Moines, IA 50319-0146
Phone: (515) 281-5294
Fax: (515) 242-5988
http://www.state.ia.us/educate/index.html
* *http://www.state.ia.us/educate/ecese/nclb/doc/*
   ccsb.html

Kansas State Department of Education
120 SE Tenth Avenue
Topeka, KS 66612-1182
Phone: (785) 296-3201
Fax: (785) 296-7933
http://www.ksbe.state.ks.us/Welcome.html
* *http://www.ksbe.state.ks.us/assessment/
   index.html*

Kentucky Department of Education
500 Mero Street
Frankfort, KY 40601
Phone: (502) 564-4770 or (800) 533-5372
TTY: (502) 564-4970
http://www.education.ky.gov/

Louisiana Department of Education
P.O. Box 94064
Baton Rouge, LA 70804-9064
Phone: (877) 453-2721
http://www.doe.state.la.us/lde/index.html
* *http://www.doe.state.la.us/doecd/reaching.asp*

Maine Department of Education
23 State House Station
Augusta, ME 04333-0023
Phone: (207) 624-6774
Fax: (207) 624-6771
http://www.state.me.us/education/
* *http://www.state.me.us/education/lsalt/
   compassess.htm*

Maryland State Department of Education
200 West Baltimore Street
Baltimore, MD 21201
Phone: (410) 767-0100
http://marylandpublicschools.org/
* *http://mdk12.org/*

Massachusetts Department of Education
350 Main Street
Malden, MA 02148-5023
Phone: (781) 338-3000
http://www.doe.mass.edu/
* *http://www.doe.mass.edu/frameworks/current.html*

Michigan Department of Education
608 West Allegan
Lansing, MI 48933
Phone: (517) 373-3324
http://michigan.gov/mde/

Minnesota Department of Education
1500 Highway 36 West
Roseville, MN 55113-4266
Phone: (651) 582-8200
*http://www.education.state.mn.us/html/mde_
home.htm*

Mississippi Department of Education
Central High School
P.O. Box 771
359 North West Street
Jackson, MS 39205
Phone: (601) 359-3513
http://www.mde.k12.ms.us/
* *http://marcopolo.mde.k12.ms.us/
   frameworks.html*

Missouri Department of Elementary and
   Secondary Education
P.O. Box 480
Jefferson City, MO 65102
Phone: (573) 751-4212
Fax: (573) 751-8613
http://www.dese.state.mo.us/
* *http://www.dese.state.mo.us/standards/*

Montana Office of Public Instruction
P.O. Box 202501
Helena, MT 59620-2501
Phone: (406) 444-3095 or (888) 231-9393
http://www.opi.state.mt.us/
* *http://www.opi.state.mt.us/Standards/Index.html*

Nebraska Department of Education
301 Centennial Mall South
Lincoln, NE 68509
Phone: (402) 471-2295
http://www.nde.state.ne.us/
* *http://www.nde.state.ne.us/AcadStand.html*

Nevada Department of Education
700 East Fifth Street
Carson City, NV 89701
Phone: (775) 687-9200
Fax: (775) 687-9101
http://www.nde.state.nv.us/
* *http://www.nde.state.nv.us/sca/standards/
index.html*

New Hampshire Department of Education
101 Pleasant Street
Concord, NH 03301-3860
Phone: (603) 271-3494
Fax: (603) 271-1953
http://www.ed.state.nh.us/
* *http://www.ed.state.nh.us/Curriculum
Frameworks/curricul.htm*

New Jersey Department of Education
P.O. Box 500
Trenton, NJ 08625
Phone: (609) 292-4469
http://www.state.nj.us/education/index.html
* *http://www.state.nj.us/njded/stass/index.html*

New Mexico Public Education Department
300 Don Gaspar
Santa Fe, NM 87501-2786
Phone: (505) 827-5800
http://www.sde.state.nm.us/
* *http://164.64.166.11/cilt/standards/*

New York State Education Department
89 Washington Avenue
Albany, NY 12234
Phone: (518) 474-3852
http://www.nysed.gov/home.html
* *http://www.nysatl.nysed.gov/standards.html*

North Carolina Department of
Public Instruction
301 North Wilmington Street
Raleigh, NC 27601
Phone: (919) 807-3300
http://www.ncpublicschools.org/
* *http://www.ncpublicschools.org/curriculum/*

North Dakota Department of
Public Instruction
600 East Boulevard Avenue
Department 201
Floors 9, 10, and 11
Bismarck, ND 58505-0440
Phone: (701) 328-2260
Fax: (701) 328-2461
http://www.dpi.state.nd.us/index.shtm
* *http://www.dpi.state.nd.us/standard/index.shtm*

Ohio Department of Education
25 South Front Street
Columbus, OH 43215-4183
Phone: (877) 644-6338
http://www.ode.state.oh.us/
* *http://www.ode.state.oh.us/academic_
content_standards/*

Oklahoma State Department of Education
2500 North Lincoln Boulevard
Oklahoma City, OK 73105-4599
Phone: (405) 521-3301
Fax: (405) 521-6205
http://www.sde.state.ok.us/home/defaultie.html

Oregon Department of Education
255 Capitol Street NE
Salem, OR 97310-0203
Phone: (503) 378-3569
TDD: (503) 378-2892
Fax: (503) 378-5156
http://www.ode.state.or.us/
* *http://www.ode.state.or.us/asmt/standards/*

Pennsylvania Department of Education
333 Market Street
Harrisburg, PA 17126
Phone: (717) 783-6788
*http://www.pde.state.pa.us/pde_internet/site/
default.asp*
* *http://www.pde.state.pa.us/stateboard_ed/
cwp/view.asp?a=3&Q=76716&stateboard_
edNav=|5467|*

Rhode Island Department of Education
255 Westminster Street
Providence, RI 02903
Phone: (401) 222-4600
http://www.ridoe.net/
* *http://www.ridoe.net/standards/frameworks/*
  default.htm

South Carolina Department of Education
1429 Senate Street
Columbia, SC 29201
Phone: (803) 734-8815
Fax: (803) 734-3389
http://www.myscschools.com/
* *http://www.myscschools.com/offices/cso/*

South Dakota Department of Education
700 Governors Drive
Pierre, SD 57501
http://www.state.sd.us/deca/Index.htm
* *http://www.state.sd.us/deca/OCTA/*
  contentstandards/index.htm

Tennessee Department of Education
Andrew Johnson Tower, 6th Floor
Nashville, TN 37243-0375
Phone: (615) 741-2731
http://www.state.tn.us/education/
* *http://www.state.tn.us/education/ci/*
  cistandards.htm

Texas Education Agency
1701 North Congress Avenue
Austin, TX 78701
Phone: (512) 463-9734
http://www.tea.state.tx.us/
* *http://www.tea.state.tx.us/teks/index.html*
* *http://www.tea.state.tx.us/student.assessment/*
  teachers.html

Utah State Office of Education
250 East 500 South
P.O. Box 144200
Salt Lake City, UT 84114-4200
Phone: (801) 538-7500
http://www.usoe.k12.ut.us/
* *http://www.uen.org/core/*

Vermont Department of Education
120 State Street
Montpelier, VT 05620-2501
http://www.state.vt.us/educ/
* *http://www.state.vt.us/educ/new/html/pubs/*
  framework.html

Virginia Department of Education
P.O. Box 2120
Richmond, VA 23218
Phone: (800) 292-3820
http://www.pen.k12.va.us/
* *http://www.pen.k12.va.us/VDOE/Instruction/*
  sol.html

Washington Office of the Superintendent
   of Public Instruction (OSPI)
Old Capitol Building
P.O. Box 47200
Olympia, WA 98504-7200
Phone: (360) 725-6000
TTY: (360) 664-3631
http://www.k12.wa.us/
* *http://www.k12.wa.us/curriculuminstruct/*

West Virginia Department of Education
1900 Kanawha Boulevard East
Charleston, WV 25305
Phone: (304) 558-3660
Fax: (304) 558-0198
http://wvde.state.wv.us/
* *http://wvde.state.wv.us/csos/*

Wisconsin Department of Public Instruction
125 South Webster Street
P.O. Box 7841
Madison, WI 53707-7841
Phone: (608) 266-3390 or (800) 441-4563
http://www.dpi.state.wi.us/index.html
* *http://www.dpi.state.wi.us/dpi/dlsis/currinst.html*

Wyoming Department of Education
2300 Capitol Avenue
Hathaway Building, 2nd Floor
Cheyenne, WY 82002-0050
Phone: (307) 777-7675
Fax: (307) 777-6234
http://www.k12.wy.us/index.asp
* *http://www.k12.wy.us/eqa/nca/pubs/*
  standards.asp

Introducing the Tests to Your Students

Before tackling any new task, it is a good idea to come up with a game plan for how to proceed. Figuring out a game plan and conveying it to your students can make the task of test taking seem more manageable and even fun!

This book outlines the steps for developing a test-preparation game plan and gives you the tools you will need along the way, including innovative activities and sample test questions. However, the approach you use in preparing your students will be key to their success. This book's game plan is designed to draw upon your strengths as an encouraging and motivating teacher—in short, as a testing "coach."

Adopting the role of a coach will aid you in helping your students overcome obstacles they face in preparing for state tests. Since these tests are not usually the most enjoyable experiences for students, using the "coach approach" can help eliminate test anxiety, build confidence, develop skills, and increase motivation.

This chapter will explain how to get students started off on the right foot by presenting state standardized tests as important challenges that students can train for together as a team.

The Coach Approach

The activities in this book are designed to build upon and enhance skills that are assessed on state standardized tests in a way that is active, engaging, stimulating, and fun. Remember—test preparation does not have to be boring. Move beyond the usual "skill and drill" and get creative in your approach to teaching. Put on your coach's cap and get your students excited about achieving their test-taking goals.

Coaching can be viewed as the application of teaching strategies to a set of activities that introduce, reinforce, and synthesize skills that players (students) need in order to perform their best. The role involves juggling many tasks at once. As a coach, you are an instructor, a facilitator, a motivator, a troubleshooter, and a supporter, all in one. The role also implies a strong desire to do the job and do it well.

As a good coach, you will motivate your students to do their best, giving them the confidence to work on skills that need improvement. Coaching is a long-term process, requiring both dedication and flexibility. A successful coach will be:

- ✗ Patient
- ✗ Positive
- ✗ Motivated
- ✗ Resourceful
- ✗ Creative

Devising a Game Plan

A good coach plans ahead in order to prepare the team for victory. After you have determined your individual approach to coaching, the next step is to develop a game plan. A successful game plan will include activities and exercises targeted to the particular needs of the team. By focusing on areas where students need a boost, you will help them evolve from a scrappy set of inexperienced players to an accomplished team of testing aces. Here is an overview of the instructional game plan outlined in this book:

- ✗ Assess students' abilities through diagnostic tests (Chapter 3).
- ✗ Set realistic goals for the team based on the diagnostic results.
- ✗ Use these goals to develop objectives for skill development.
- ✗ Strengthen these skills by using specific reading and math activities (Chapters 5 and 7).
- ✗ Involve the team in new approaches that use more than one skill at a time (Chapters 5 and 7).
- ✗ Simulate the game environment through test scrimmages and practice testing scenarios (Chapters 3, 6, and 8).
- ✗ Incorporate strategies that help boost skills and performance (Chapter 4).
- ✗ Evaluate the process and teach students how to evaluate what they are doing (Chapter 4).

Before devising a training program, the coach must discern where the players are and where they need to go in order to be successful. That is why we recommend starting your program with the checklist and diagnostic tests in Chapter 3. By first assessing your students' skills and their familiarity with the format of standardized tests, you will be able to formulate an appropriate and realistic plan to help them best prepare for the tests ahead. Using this plan, you can then select suitable activities to work on particular skills and present meaningful strategies for students to apply during the tests.

When introducing your state's tests to students, establish your role as coach from the beginning. Explain that you will be working with the students to figure out where they are in order to get them where they should be before the "big games" that lie ahead. Make it clear that along the way, you will be showing them several strategies they can use in their weaker areas when they feel trapped with the ball, so to speak.

Describe the tests not as something impossible to beat, but as something students can handle on their own. The training program you are developing, based on the students' "pre-event trials" (the diagnostic tests in Chapter 3), will help prepare them well for the tests. Explain that you will also help them stay motivated and maintain a positive attitude toward the tests throughout the program. Make it clear that you welcome any ideas they may have to make the process more fun and less tedious.

Cross Training in the Classroom

Since you want to avoid burnout that can happen through basic drill instruction, and since you are an innovative coach by nature, try cross training your academic athletes.

In the usual sense, cross training means varying a regular exercise routine with different forms of exercise to reach the same goal. For example, soccer players may lift weights, football players may take up ballet, and runners may try bicycling to vary their workouts. These different types of activities give athletes new strengths and skills that make them better at their primary sports.

Cross training is an important facet of the coaching philosophy. It can easily be applied to training your students to face testing challenges. Drilling students with practice questions is an important part of test preparation, but it can become monotonous and boring. Cross training can keep students from getting bored. If students are given a variety of methods for developing testing skills, they will learn to apply their skills in different contexts, adapt their strategies to different activities, and synthesize these skills and strategies more naturally when performing on tests. Chapters 4, 5, and 7 of this book address methods of cross training and provide ways to change up the normal "training program" for your students. Here are a few suggestions taken from those chapters:

X   Intermingle straight drills with activities.

X   Use different or unusual content to teach skills that cross disciplines. (For example, rather than using a story to teach students how to find the main idea, try a popular song, magazine ad, or science article instead.)

X   Engage students in activities that practice and develop more than one skill at a time.

X   Set aside some time to teach students methods they can use to deal with test anxiety.

X   Mix it up skillwise. Rather than concentrating on reading standards for weeks on end, slip in a math-oriented activity or something that deals with other standards your students are learning in school.

X   Take a break from training. Avoid overtraining by planning "rest days" when the goal is to have fun learning something new or to try something different.

A beginning team may need to start with simple objectives before moving up to the goal of winning or defeating the opponent. From this standpoint, a good coaching strategy involves building on individual skills incrementally. Having students exercise several skills at once can also help keep tedium on the sidelines while encouraging a more integrated application that reflects the real world. This book provides some activities that focus on just one particular standard or skill, as well as others that tie related skills together in integrated ways.

The Mental Game: Motivation, Metacognition, and Modeling

One of the most important aspects of coaching is motivation. Motivated students have an edge when faced with any academic challenge. Give your students plenty of compelling reasons to want to do well on state tests, and boost their self-confidence by preparing them thoroughly. If they see a reason to do well and believe they can learn the necessary skills, students will be well prepared and focused on testing days.

Coaching also involves constant evaluation—of progress, of problems, and of the process itself. Helping students develop metacognitive skills, or making them aware of their own processes and progress, will pay off enormously. Use the test-taking strategies in Chapter 4 to teach your students how to think about what they are doing while they are doing it and to identify their own strengths and weaknesses. Encourage them to use their minds to reduce anxiety and alleviate fears about testing. Using metacognition throughout the test-preparation process will help students stay focused and remain in control during the tests.

Another way to help students psych themselves up for testing is to model a positive attitude toward the process. Try not to let any frustrations you may have about the tests dampen your students' motivation. As a coach, you should remain positive and encouraging during training. Encourage team spirit by talking about each test as a big game. Explain that you are going to prepare the students by giving them the techniques, strategies, and experiences needed to give a peak performance. And when introducing the activities in this book, describe exactly how they will help students become better, stronger test-takers.

Standardized tests are a fact a life for students today. Those bound for college will encounter even more high-stakes tests. Your job as a coach is to teach students how to tackle those tests with confidence. You can remove the often crippling obstacles of anxiety and uncertainty from your students' paths, but it will take some work. The activities, strategies, and sample tests in this book, coupled with your own persistence and creativity as a coach, will all work together to boost students' skills and confidence.

How Coaching Looks in the Classroom

Since coaching is an active and involved role, any instruction related to your state's standardized tests should be, too. The activities in this book reflect this hands-on approach and provide lots of modeling potential. Each activity has been broken down into the following categories, allowing you to guide students through it step-by-step: Skills/State Standards, Description, Materials You Need, Getting Ready, Introducing the Activity, Modeling the Activity, Activity in Practice, and Extensions.

The activities are designed for collaborative pair or group work. However, many are adaptable and can be used with individual students for more focused skill instruction. No matter how you decide to use them, the activities are student-centered in nature, allowing you, the coach, to facilitate and assess while students actively develop their skills.

Identifying Problem Areas

In order to develop a program that will bring your students to peak performance on state assessment tests, begin by identifying any problem areas in their skill development. This will save you time and energy in the long run, and make the whole experience of preparing for the tests more advantageous for students. The short reading and math tests included in this chapter are representative of sixth-grade state assessment tests. They can be used as diagnostic tools to help pinpoint areas in which students need work.

Before administering these diagnostic tests, it may be helpful to determine what exposure your students have had to the look, feel, and content of your state's tests. Think about what they do in the classroom that addresses test preparation in some way. Since your state's standards serve as the scaffolding for the curriculum, students should already be learning the content and developing the skills that will be assessed on the tests. However, they may not realize that what they are learning directly connects to the tests they will take. Use the following checklist of questions to review the key elements of the tests in connection with your students' current testing knowledge.

Checklist: Evaluating Your Students' Testing Savvy

General Questions

☐ Do students have experience with multiple-choice tests?

☐ How often do students read or write silently in class?

☐ How often do students take tests individually?

☐ What forms of standardized tests have students taken this year or previously?

☐ Have students had practice using answer sheets to record their answers?

Reading Questions

☐ How often do students read expository texts? (articles, interviews, biographies, personal narratives, etc.)

☐ What types of literature do students read most frequently? (short stories, novels, poetry, plays, etc.)

☐ How often do students read aloud?

☐ How familiar are students with alternative forms of text? (advertisements, Web sites, written directions, pamphlets, etc.)

☐ How often do students read texts for different purposes? (entertainment, skimming for facts, answering questions, etc.)

Reading Questions *(continued)*

- ☐ What literary devices can students identify? (foreshadowing, mood, tone, similes, symbols, alliteration, metaphors, sensory images, etc.)
- ☐ Can students distinguish between fact and opinion?
- ☐ Can students use reference books?
- ☐ Can students use text features such as table of contents, indexes, and illustrations?
- ☐ What story elements can students identify? (plot, setting, character, problem/conflict, resolution, theme, etc.)
- ☐ Can students analyze character, including traits, motives, conflicts, and changes?
- ☐ Do students use context clues to determine meanings of words?
- ☐ Can students identify prefixes, suffixes, and root words?
- ☐ Can students find the main idea and supporting details in a text?
- ☐ Do students understand the use of comparison and contrast?
- ☐ Can students identify an author's purpose?
- ☐ Do students understand cause and effect?

Writing Questions

- ☐ How often do students use lists or graphic organizers to prepare for writing?
- ☐ How often do students write in response to texts they have read?
- ☐ What are the most frequent forms of writing done by students?
- ☐ Are students comfortable with both creative and expository writing?
- ☐ Can students use facts, details, and personal experiences to support their opinions?
- ☐ Do students understand the purpose of a first draft?
- ☐ How often do students revise their writing?
- ☐ How often do students use dictionaries or thesauruses during the writing process?
- ☐ How often do students use literary devices in their writing?
- ☐ How often do students draw upon their own experiences in their writing?
- ☐ Can students apply a variety of spelling strategies?
- ☐ Do students use the conventions of punctuation?
- ☐ For what occasions and purposes do students typically write? (letters to invite or thank, information to record, creative writing to entertain or express, etc.)
- ☐ Can students use computers to create, revise, retrieve, and check information?

Math Questions

- ☐ How familiar are students with comparing and ordering rational numbers?
- ☐ How often do students use fractions, decimals, and percents?
- ☐ How often do students use addition and subtraction?
- ☐ How often do students use multiplication and division?
- ☐ How familiar are students with word problems?
- ☐ Can students identify and extend numerical and geometric patterns to make predictions and solve problems?
- ☐ Can students identify patterns in pictorial models?
- ☐ How often do students use lists, tables, and charts to express patterns and relationships?
- ☐ Can students name, describe, and compare shapes and solids using formal geometric vocabulary?
- ☐ Can students identify congruent shapes and identify lines of symmetry?
- ☐ How often do students use number lines?
- ☐ How often do students use rulers to measure?
- ☐ Can students read clocks for time and thermometers for temperature?
- ☐ Can students convert units within the same system?
- ☐ Can students convert units between customary and metric systems?
- ☐ How often do students use graphs?
- ☐ How often do students work with mean, median, and mode?
- ☐ How often do students create formulas and equations?
- ☐ Are students familiar with ratios and proportions?
- ☐ Are students used to rounding and estimating?
- ☐ Can students use information given in sequence to determine missing information or identify patterns?
- ☐ Can students use logical reasoning to solve problems?

For a tailor-made checklist based on your state's standards, see the information provided by your state's education department or agency on the language arts and math standards for grade six. The Web site addresses at the end of Chapter 1 (pages 8–12) should provide links to lists of standards available on-line.

Diagnostic Reading Test—Grade 6

Directions: Read the following excerpt from the story. Then, answer questions 1 through 10 on your answer sheet.

The Happy Prince

Adapted from The Happy Prince *by Oscar Wilde (originally published in 1888)*

Notes about the reading

(1) High above the city, on a tall column, stood the statue of the Happy Prince. He was gilded all over with thin leaves of fine gold. For eyes he had two bright sapphires, and a large red ruby glowed on his sword hilt.

(2) The Happy Prince was very much admired. "He is as beautiful as a weathercock," remarked one of the town councillors who wished to gain a reputation for having artistic tastes. "Only not quite so useful," he added, fearing lest people should think him unpractical, which he really was not.

(3) "Why can't you be like the Happy Prince?" asked a sensible mother of her little boy who was crying for the moon. "The Happy Prince never dreams of crying for anything."

(4) "I am glad there is someone in the world who is quite happy," muttered a disappointed man as he gazed at the wonderful statue.

(5) "He looks just like an angel," said the charity children as they came out of the cathedral in their bright scarlet cloaks and clean white pinafores.

(6) "How do you know?" said the mathematical master. "You have never seen one."

(7) "Ah! But we have, in our dreams," answered the children. The mathematical master frowned and looked very severe, for he did not approve of children dreaming.

(8) One night there flew over the city a little swallow. His friends had gone away to Egypt six weeks before, but he had stayed behind, for he was in love with the most beautiful reed. He had met her early in the spring as he was flying down the river after a big yellow moth. He had been so attracted by her slender waist that he had stopped to talk to her.

Notes about the reading

(9) "Shall I love you?" said the swallow, who liked to come to the point at once, and the reed made him a low bow. He flew round and round her, touching the water with his wings and making silver ripples. This was his courtship, and it lasted all through the summer.

(10) "It is a ridiculous attachment," twittered the other swallows. "She has no money and far too many relations." And, indeed, the river was quite full of reeds. Then, when the autumn came, the other swallows all flew away.

(11) After they had gone, the little swallow felt lonely and began to tire of his ladylove. "She has no conversation," he said, "and I am afraid that she is a **coquette**, for she is always flirting with the wind." And, certainly, whenever the wind blew, the reed made the most graceful curtsies. "I admit that she is domestic," he continued, "but I love traveling, and my wife, consequently, should love traveling also."

(12) "Will you come away with me?" he said finally to her. But the reed shook her head, she was so attached to her home.

(13) "You have been trifling with me!" he cried. "I am off to the Pyramids. Good-bye!" And with that, the swallow flew away.

(14) All day long he flew, and at nighttime he arrived at the city. "Where shall I put up?" he said. "I hope the town has made preparations."

(15) Just then, he saw the statue on the tall column. "I will put up there," he cried. "It is a fine position with plenty of fresh air." He alighted just between the feet of the Happy Prince.

(16) "I have a golden bedroom," the swallow said softly to himself as he looked round, and he prepared to go to sleep. But just as he was putting his head under his wing, a large drop of water fell on him. "What a curious thing!" he cried. "There is not a single cloud in the sky, the stars are quite clear and bright, and yet it is raining. The climate in the north of Europe is really dreadful. The reed used to like the rain, but that was merely her selfishness."

Diagnostic Reading Test—Grade 6 (continued)

Notes about the reading

(17) Then, another drop fell.

(18) "What is the use of a statue if it cannot keep the rain off?" the swallow cried. "I must look for a good chimney pot," he said and determined to fly away.

(19) But before he had opened his wings, a third drop fell. He looked up and saw— ah! what did he see?

(20) The eyes of the Happy Prince were filled with tears, and tears were running down his golden cheeks. His face was so beautiful in the moonlight that the little swallow was filled with pity.

(21) "Who are you?" the swallow said.

(22) "I am the Happy Prince."

(23) "Why are you weeping then?" asked the swallow. "You have quite drenched me."

(24) "When I was alive and had a human heart," answered the statue, "I did not know what tears were, for I lived in the Palace of Sans-Souci, where sorrow is not allowed to enter. In the daytime, I played with my companions in the garden. In the evening, I led the dance in the Great Hall. Round the garden ran a very lofty wall, but I never cared to ask what lay beyond it—everything about me was so beautiful. My courtiers called me the Happy Prince, and happy indeed I was, if pleasure be happiness. So I lived, and so I died. And now that I am dead, they have set me up here so high that I can see all of the ugliness and misery of my city, and though my heart is made of lead, I cannot choose but weep."

(25) "What, is he not solid gold?" said the swallow to himself. He was too polite to make any personal remarks out loud.

Notes about the reading

(26)   "Far away," continued the statue in a low musical voice, "far away in a little street, there is a poor house. One of the windows is open, and through it I can see a woman seated at a table. Her face is thin and worn, and she has coarse red hands, all pricked by the needle, for she is a seamstress. She is embroidering passionflowers on a satin gown for the loveliest of the Queen's maids of honor to wear at the next ball. In a bed in the corner of the room, her little boy is lying ill. He has a fever and is asking for oranges. His mother has nothing to give him but river water, so he is crying. Swallow, swallow, little swallow, will you not bring her the ruby out of my sword hilt? My feet are fastened to this pedestal and I cannot move."

(27)   "I am waited for in Egypt," said the swallow. "My friends are flying up and down the Nile and talking to the large lotus flowers. Soon, they will go to sleep in the tomb of the great King. The King is there himself in his painted coffin. He is wrapped in yellow linen and embalmed with spices. Round his neck is a chain of pale green jade, and his hands are like withered leaves."

(28)   "Swallow, swallow, little swallow," said the Prince, "will you not stay with me for one night and be my messenger? The boy is so thirsty and the mother so sad."

(29)   "I don't think I like boys," answered the swallow. "Last summer, when I was staying on the river, there were two rude boys, the miller's sons, who were always throwing stones at me. They never hit me, of course. We swallows fly far too well for that, and besides, I come from a family famous for its **agility**. But still, it was a mark of disrespect."

(30)   But the Happy Prince looked so sad that the little swallow was sorry. "It is very cold here," he said, "but I will stay with you for one night and be your messenger."

(31)   "Thank you, little swallow," said the Prince.

(32)   So the swallow picked out the great ruby from the Prince's sword and flew away with it in his beak over the roofs of the town.

Diagnostic Reading Test—Grade 6 (continued)

1 Why does the swallow initially stay in the city when his friends go to Egypt?

   A He dislikes warm weather.

   B He likes his home on the statue.

   C He is in love with a plant.

   D He has injured his right wing.

2 What is the attitude of the townspeople toward the statue?

   F resentful

   G admiring

   H indifferent

   J confident

3 In paragraph 11, which word helps the reader know what **coquette** means?

   A "conversation"

   B "ladylove"

   C "traveling"

   D "flirting"

4 Paragraph 26 is mostly about—

   F a family that needs help.

   G the Prince's palace life.

   H the charms of travel in Egypt.

   J how the swallow met the Prince.

5 The swallow is surprised to learn that the Prince—

   A was once rich and happy.

   B is not made entirely of gold.

   C can see faraway houses.

   D loved an enemy princess.

6 Why does the Prince cry in paragraphs 16–23?

   F He is annoyed that the swallow has landed on him.

   G He is frustrated because he has to give up a ruby.

   H He sees sadness and misery in the human world.

   J He freezes and bakes due to the wind and sun.

GO ON

Diagnostic Reading Test—Grade 6 (continued)

7 What is the BEST evidence that the swallow has a kind heart?

    A He flies in circles around the reed.

    B He brings gifts to his friends in Egypt.

    C He seeks out a warm place for the night.

    D He agrees to stay and help the Prince.

8 What is the BEST antonym for the word **agility** as used in paragraph 29?

    F skill

    G talent

    H clumsiness

    J nobility

9 Which word BEST describes the author's tone?

    A fearful

    B lighthearted

    C regretful

    D joyous

10 SHORT ANSWER: Answer the following question on your answer sheet. Use complete sentences.

Based on the part of the story you have read, what do you predict will happen next? Support your answer with evidence from the text.

GO ON

Directions: Read the Web page. Then, answer questions 11 through 15 on your answer sheet.

Visit Angel Falls

Angel Falls is the highest waterfall on Earth. It lies in eastern Venezuela in Canaima National Park. Starting from *Auyán-tepuí*, or Devil's Mountain, it plunges nearly 3,212 feet (979 m) into the *Cañón del Diablo*, or Devil's Canyon. This immense and amazing natural wonder is about 20 times higher than Niagara Falls!

The local Pemon Indians call the falls *Kerepakupai-merú*, which means "falls from the deepest place." Venezuelans call the waterfall *Salto Ángel*. However, you might be surprised to learn that the falls were not named for heavenly, winged creatures. They were named for an American pilot and adventurer, Jimmie Angel.

Jimmie Angel first sighted the falls in 1935. He thought that the surrounding area contained a lost river of gold. In 1937, he returned with his small four-seater plane to search for gold near *Auyán-tepuí*. He landed on top of the mountain, but his plane got stuck in a boggy marsh and could not take off again. Jimmie, his wife, and two other travelers had to hike for days through the jungle to get back to their camp. Their plane remained on the mountain for the next 33 years.

Flat-topped mountains known as *tepuis* surround Angel Falls. These "table mountains" have nearly vertical sides and add to the dramatic landscape. The waters fall freely from cliffs and reach the bottom of the valley as a rush of misty spray. These waters gather into a small creek, which eventually becomes the Churún River, which flows north.

A trip to Angel Falls is an exciting adventure. There is no way to reach the falls by road. Many visitors start at the charming village of Canaima, which lies about 30 miles (50 km) to the northwest of the falls. We can help you make plans to fly to Canaima and then take a small plane or boat to see the magnificent falls. Your visit is sure to be unforgettable!

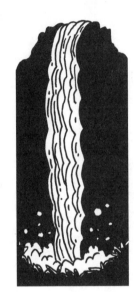

Click here to find out about **inoculations** and health advice.

Click here to find out about **flights** to Caracas and on to Canaima.

Click here to check out the latest **exchange rates** for Venezuela.

Venezuela
Canaima ———
Canaima National Park   Angel Falls

We can help you decide how to experience the beauty of Angel Falls. There are several ways to reach the falls.

- Hike on foot through spectacular wilderness.

- Fly over the falls in a helicopter.

- Rent a plane.

- Paddle up the river in a *curiara*, or dugout canoe.

Call **888-555-7890** to find out more about Angel Falls.

GO ON ➡

11 This Web site was written mainly to—

   F explain how *tepuis* are formed.

   G tell where to fly to in Venezuela.

   H get people to visit Angel Falls.

   J tell the story of Jimmie Angel.

12 Which sentence describes a FACT stated on the Web site?

   A Angel Falls is the highest waterfall in the world.

   B *Tepuis* add to the dramatic beauty of the land.

   C Canaima is the only village near Angel Falls.

   D Jimmie Angel was a talented pilot.

13 The site includes links to information about all of the following EXCEPT—

   F flights to Venezuela.

   G current exchange rates.

   H important health information.

   J other waterfalls in South America.

14 According to the Web site, how can people get to Angel Falls from Canaima?

   A by train

   B by car

   C by boat

   D by bus

15 Read this sentence from the Web site.

There are several ways to reach the falls.

Which sentence below uses the word **reach** with the same meaning as it is used in the sentence above?

   F Aldo began to reach for the apple to give it to Eva.

   G Diana was able to reach the village before evening.

   H Sam wanted to reach a new audience with his song.

   J Kim could not reach Lee by phone.

END OF PRACTICE TEST

Diagnostic Reading Test—Grade 6
Answer Sheet

Directions: Record your answers on this answer sheet. Be sure to fill in each bubble completely and erase any stray marks. Use the lines provided to write your short-answer response.

1 Ⓐ Ⓑ Ⓒ Ⓓ

2 Ⓕ Ⓖ Ⓗ Ⓙ

3 Ⓐ Ⓑ Ⓒ Ⓓ

4 Ⓕ Ⓖ Ⓗ Ⓙ

5 Ⓐ Ⓑ Ⓒ Ⓓ

6 Ⓕ Ⓖ Ⓗ Ⓙ

7 Ⓐ Ⓑ Ⓒ Ⓓ

8 Ⓕ Ⓖ Ⓗ Ⓙ

9 Ⓐ Ⓑ Ⓒ Ⓓ

10 SHORT ANSWER: Use the space below to answer the question in complete sentences.

Based on the part of the story you have read, what do you predict will happen next? Support your answer with evidence from the text.

_____

_____

_____

_____

_____

_____

_____

_____

_____

_____

_____

11 Ⓕ Ⓖ Ⓗ Ⓙ

12 Ⓐ Ⓑ Ⓒ Ⓓ

13 Ⓕ Ⓖ Ⓗ Ⓙ

14 Ⓐ Ⓑ Ⓒ Ⓓ

15 Ⓕ Ⓖ Ⓗ Ⓙ

Diagnostic Math Test—Grade 6

Directions: Read and solve each problem. Record your answers on your answer sheet.

1   A biologist counts the number of bacteria in a petri dish. Her findings are recorded in the chart below.

Population of Bacteria

Time	Number of Bacteria
1:00 P.M.	5
2:00 P.M.	10
3:00 P.M.	20
4:00 P.M.	40

If the pattern continues, how many bacteria will be in the dish at 7:00 P.M.?

A   160

B   240

C   320

D   640

2   Falen earns $6 an hour baby-sitting. Which expression describes the number of hours, H, that Falen will have to baby-sit to earn at least $36?

F $H = 4$ hours

G $H > 5$ hours

H $H \geq 6$ hours

J $H < 36$ hours

3   The circumference of a circle is 32.51 cm. What is the approximate length of the circle's radius?

A   4 cm

B   5 cm

C   6 cm

D   7 cm

4   The table below compares Martin's age with his grandfather's age.

Age Comparison

Martin	Grandfather
3	68
5	70
8	73
10	75

Let m represent Martin's age and g represent his grandfather's age. Which equation shows the relationship between their ages?

F $m = g + 65$

G $g = m - 63$

H $m = g - 63$

J $g = m + 65$

GO ON ➡

5 A quarter is tossed two times in a row. Which table shows all of the possible outcomes for the two tosses?

A

First Toss	Second Toss
heads	heads
tails	tails

B

First Toss	Second Toss
heads	heads
tails	heads
heads	tails
tails	tails

C

First Toss	Second Toss
heads	tails
tails	heads
heads	tails
tails	heads

D

First Toss	Second Toss
tails	tails
heads	tails
heads	heads

6 One angle of an isosceles triangle is 70° and the other two angles are congruent. Which method can be used to find the measure of one of the congruent angles?

F Subtract 70 from 180 and then divide by 2.

G Add 70 to 180 and then divide by 3.

H Divide 70 by 2 and then subtract from 180.

J Multiply 70 by 2 and then add 180.

7 One side of a cube measures 14 inches. Find its volume.

A 2,744 in.^{3}

B 3,158 in.^{3}

C 4,600 in.^{3}

D 4,844 in.^{3}

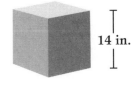

14 in.

8 If Roman correctly marked 0.14, $^4/_2$, 0.041, and $^1/_4$ on a number line, which number would be closest to zero?

F 0.14

G $^4/_2$

H 0.041

J $^1/_4$

GO ON

9 By the middle of January, 25% of Ms. Cantrill's class had completed a long-term art project. What fraction of the class had NOT yet finished?

A $^1/_{75}$

B $^1/_4$

C $^2/_7$

D $^3/_4$

10 The side lengths and areas of some regular polygons are shown in the table below.

Regular Polygons

Side Length	Area
4	16
5	25
8	64
9	81

Which geometric figure is represented by the information in the table?

F triangle

G hexagon

H dodecagon

J square

11 Mr. Witty recorded these scores for his sixth-grade language arts students.

65, 66, 68, 71, 77, 77, 77, 79, 80, 84, 84, 89, 90, 91, 91, 92, 100

What is the median of these test scores?

A 77

B 78

C 80

D 82

12 Which point on the grid represents the location of the ordered pair (4, 2)?

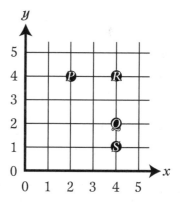

F Point P

G Point Q

H Point R

J Point S

GO ON

Diagnostic Math Test—Grade 6 (continued)

13 Laird has 5 blue balloons, 8 red balloons, 8 green ballons, and 4 orange balloons. If he lets go of one of them at random, what is the probability that he will let go of a blue balloon?

A $\frac{1}{3}$

B $\frac{1}{5}$

C $\frac{2}{7}$

D $\frac{2}{15}$

14 There were 20 llamas and 40 people registered for a llama race. Which ratio accurately compares the number of people to the number of llamas?

F 2:4

G 2:1

H 10:25

J 20:40

15 The table below shows the favorite fruits of students at Camp Fun.

Favorite Fruits

Fruit	Number of Students
Apple	30
Banana	10
Orange	55
Peach	5

Which circle graph best displays the data from the table?

A

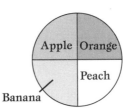

B

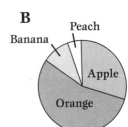

C

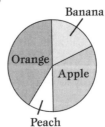

D

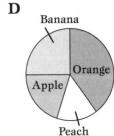

END OF PRACTICE TEST

Diagnostic Math Test—Grade 6
Answer Sheet

Directions: Record your answers on this answer sheet. Be sure to fill in each bubble completely and erase any stray marks.

1 Ⓐ Ⓑ Ⓒ Ⓓ

2 Ⓕ Ⓖ Ⓗ Ⓙ

3 Ⓐ Ⓑ Ⓒ Ⓓ

4 Ⓕ Ⓖ Ⓗ Ⓙ

5 Ⓐ Ⓑ Ⓒ Ⓓ

6 Ⓕ Ⓖ Ⓗ Ⓙ

7 Ⓐ Ⓑ Ⓒ Ⓓ

8 Ⓕ Ⓖ Ⓗ Ⓙ

9 Ⓐ Ⓑ Ⓒ Ⓓ

10 Ⓕ Ⓖ Ⓗ Ⓙ

11 Ⓐ Ⓑ Ⓒ Ⓓ

12 Ⓕ Ⓖ Ⓗ Ⓙ

13 Ⓐ Ⓑ Ⓒ Ⓓ

14 Ⓕ Ⓖ Ⓗ Ⓙ

15 Ⓐ Ⓑ Ⓒ Ⓓ

Test-Taking Skills and Strategies

As your students' testing coach, your role is twofold: to give students the knowledge they need to do well on the tests, and to equip them with strategies they can use to refuel, relax, or refocus in order to reach the finish line.

Getting students into the right frame of mind for testing is one of the most challenging tasks facing a coach. This chapter provides guidelines on how to approach any standardized test and includes test-taking strategies your students can use. Some of your students may be taking standardized tests for the first time. Teaching them these strategies now will give them a great foundation for taking tests throughout middle school and high school. This chapter is broken down into the following sections:

- ✗ Reducing Test Anxiety
- ✗ Pacing
- ✗ Strategic Guessing
- ✗ Reading Strategies
- ✗ Writing Strategies
- ✗ Math Strategies
- ✗ Top Five Things to Remember

The boxed "Coaching Clues" that appear throughout this chapter offer suggestions for additional practice or related activities. Some of the strategies discussed may also be practiced with the help of student reproducibles. These reproducible pages are arranged by strategy beginning on page 46.

Reducing Test Anxiety

When faced with standardized tests, students may experience a range of reactions, including anxiety. There are several ways you can help your students replace test anxiety with confidence: talk about the tests, familiarize students with the test format and structure, and give students techniques for dealing with any stress or distractions that can occur during testing.

You may want to begin by asking students to reflect on their own attitudes toward tests. Discuss the different feelings the prospect of taking a test may arouse, as well as how students might deal with those feelings. Ask students to share any strategies they already use when taking tests. Discuss these strategies as a class or in small groups.

> **Coaching Clue** — Use the *Testing Questionnaire* reproducible (page 46) to help encourage students to reflect on and discuss the testing process.

The more familiar students are with the tests they will take, the less stress they will likely experience. One way to help reduce test anxiety is to make students so familiar with the test format that they are comfortable when faced with the actual tests. Here are several suggestions for ways to familiarize students with your state's tests.

Take a Good Look

Review one or more previously released benchmark or practice tests developed by your state's education department. (See Chapter 1, pages 8–12, for related resources.) Divide the class into small groups and ask each group to analyze the format, content, language, and style of the tests. Have students look specifically at the directions, types of reading passages and/or test questions, the total number of questions, and any text features, such as titles, illustrations, maps, charts, and graphs. Once all of the groups have shared their findings, review the major points about each aspect of the tests. Make a chart or poster to display as a classroom reference.

Coaching Clue — Use the *Take a Good Look* reproducible (page 47) to help guide students as they analyze your state's tests. You may want to prepare by answering the questions yourself in advance so that you can add to your students' findings where appropriate.

Be a Copycat

The sample tests in this book are all modeled on the format and content of actual state tests. Try to do the same in the classroom by designing assignments, quizzes, and tests to mimic your own state's tests. For example, if the reading passages on the state test are set in two columns per page, give students examples of texts arranged in two columns. Or, if the test includes a variety of text structures (interviews, letters, poems, Web sites, etc.), try to incorporate these same structures in your curriculum. If your state's math test uses a particular numbering font or presents graphics in a distinctive style, use those types of fonts and graphics on tests or assignments that you create.

Make It Real

All coaches know that "practice makes perfect." This can certainly be applied to test taking. The more practice students have with tests that look like the real thing, the more confident and successful they will be come testing time. With this in mind, give students an authentic simulation of the testing experience at least once before the actual tests. Use the practice tests in Chapters 6 and 8 of this book, find sample tests from your state's education department, or design your own tests with the look and feel of your state's tests.

Some schools hold simulation days where students throughout the school take benchmark or trial tests. Use these simulations as opportunities to discuss the test-taking experience. Reassure students that a low score on a practice test is nothing to worry about. Explain how this is a great opportunity to spot areas that need improvement before the actual tests. Be sure to discuss what students found hardest about the tests and what strategies they applied.

Pacing

While the majority of state standardized tests are timed, your own state's tests may not be. But regardless of time limits, pacing can play a key role in a student's testing success. Pacing can help students stay on track by helping them focus their concentration, maintain their stamina, and offset any anxiety.

To introduce the concept of pacing, have students envision the tests as a series of track-and-field events. Each part of the test is like a different event. Even if students want to get the best time or highest score for one event, pacing their energy and concentration among all the events they face will ensure a better result overall. Have them practice and employ the following strategies to bolster their endurance and even out their tempo during testing.

X-O Strategy

A steady pace ensures the best performance. However, sometimes a student will come across a question that stumps him, causing him to lose his sense of rhythm. Most students approach questions as if they have to be done in order. When they hit hard questions, they get stuck and refuse to move on. And the longer they stay stuck, the more anxious and frustrated they become. This is a strategic mistake. Students' scores and attitudes will both get a boost if they make two or three passes through a test, each time skipping questions that seem too hard and going back to them after they have tried to answer all of the other questions.

The X-O strategy is a simple way to maintain a good pace and maximize scores. When working through a section, a student should first take the time to solve or answer any questions she can. However, if she starts to struggle with a confusing problem and spends more than a few minutes on it without coming up with an answer, she should stop and mark an "X" in the margin next to the question. This is a "maybe" question. The student could probably figure out the solution if she spent some more time, but for now she needs to move on and try to answer other easier problems.

If the student comes to a question that initially makes no sense to her at all, she should mark an "O" in the margin. This is a "guessing" question. Using strategic guessing techniques can help improve the odds of the student selecting the correct answer on this type of question.

After the student has answered every question she can, she should return to the X questions first and try them again. If they still give her trouble, she should apply strategic guessing techniques, such as the process of elimination (discussed on pages 33–34), to eliminate any incorrect answers. Once some of the possible answers have been eliminated, the student can make an educated guess. After the student has tried to answer all of the X questions, she should go back to the O questions and apply the same strategic guessing techniques.

The X-O strategy keeps students from freezing up when faced with tough questions. It also encourages them to answer every question, which will ultimately help their scores.

Coaching Clue — Practice this strategy with students using the *X-O Strategy* reproducible (page 48) and a previously released benchmark or practice test.

Time-Outs

Most experts believe that the average person can only handle 45 minutes of learning new material before reaching complete absorption. This belief is the reasoning behind the "45/15" rule: after 45 minutes of study, take a 15-minute break. If this is a good method for students to use when studying, why not apply it, in a modified form, to taking a test? Tell students that one way to pace themselves during a test is to take a time-out after each section. Alternatively, they can take a break every half hour or so, stretching a bit while still at their desks. Encourage students to use the timed breaks to get up and stretch, get a drink of water, or walk around the hall a bit to refresh themselves before going back to the test.

Desk Stretches

Most state assessment tests are several hours long. Students understandably find it difficult and uncomfortable to remain in the same position for a very long time. To help students combat desk fatigue, teach them some stretches they can do while sitting at their desks. The exercises that follow are written so that you can read them directly from the page to your students.

Four-Square Neck Stretches

1. Sitting straight in your chair, tilt your head forward. Try to touch your chin to your chest. Hold for five counts.

2. Tilt your head backward and look up at the ceiling. Let the back of your head rest on the base of your neck while keeping your shoulders relaxed. Hold for five counts.

3. Tilt your head to the right, bringing your ear close to your right shoulder. Hold for five counts.

4. Tilt your head to the left, bringing your ear close to your left shoulder. Hold for five counts.

Shoulder Roll and Pull

1. While seated at your desk, roll both shoulders forward in a circular motion. Continue for a count of ten. Try to keep your neck relaxed. Concentrate on rotating your shoulders in circles rather than just lifting them straight up and down.

2. Switch direction and roll your shoulders backward, also for a count of ten.

3. Next, clasp your hands together and extend your arms out from your chest, as if you are getting ready to hit a volleyball with your forearms. Concentrate on separating your shoulder blades, pulling the muscles in your upper back away from the center and out toward your hands. Hold for five counts.

Answer Bubbles

Nearly all standardized tests require students to record their answers by filling in some form of lettered bubbles. As with anything else, the more experience students have using bubble answer sheets, the more natural the process will feel during the actual tests. Give students the practice they need by incorporating bubble-style answer grids into everyday activities, from daily warm-ups to homework review or pop quizzes.

One of the pitfalls of skipping a question in the test booklet is that a student may forget to skip that same problem on the answer sheet. Having students use simple bookmarks or rulers while testing can help them stay on top of which problems they are skipping and need to go back to later. Check your state's guidelines to see if tools like these are allowed during testing.

Another approach is to have students record their choices on the answer sheet after they have finished each section. This reduces the risk of filling in the bubbles incorrectly. Just tell students to write or circle their final answer choice for each question in the test booklet itself. Then, after each section, they can transfer their answers to the answer sheet.

Strategic Guessing

Even though state assessment exams do not normally feature a guessing penalty, this does not mean students should just guess randomly. Encourage students to use strategic guessing strategies by explaining how this can help them choose smart answers and, in turn, raise their scores.

Make it clear to your students from the start that guessing is not cheating. Even if students think they couldn't possibly know the right answer, remind them that they have multiple tools on hand to tackle every question. They can use prior knowledge and experience, as well as what they just learned by reading a passage or thinking about a problem. These tools, combined with smart guessing, can all help students figure out what the correct answer might be.

Although the X-O strategy (page 36) can help students pace themselves throughout the test, it can also be used as the first step toward guessing strategically. If students begin by answering the questions they definitely know first, they can then go back and deal with the remaining questions using smart guessing and the process of elimination.

POE: Process of Elimination

Applying POE, or the process of elimination, during a test simply means weeding out any unsuitable answer choices. The inherent beauty of multiple-choice tests is that the correct answers are always provided—students just have to learn how to identify them.

Students are often amazed and encouraged when you explain that the right answers are in plain view in their test booklets. To get students comfortable with POE, first explain that the answers are all there on the page. Then, show them how the process works. Write a sample question and answer choices, such as the following, on the board or on an overhead transparency:

About how much does an adult male forest elephant weigh?

A   30 pounds
B   200 pounds
C   2,000 pounds
D   10,000 pounds

Students can come up with a likely answer to this question very quickly using logic. Ask them to think about how much they weigh and how much members of their families weigh. Then, have them consider each of the answer choices.

- Choice A is too small. Human toddlers weigh about 30 pounds.

- Choice B is bigger, but still too small. A human adult could weigh 200 pounds, but, obviously, humans are much smaller than even the smallest of adult elephants.

- Choices C and D seem somewhat likely. They are both pretty large numbers, and students will know that an elephant must weigh a lot. If they had to make educated guesses at this point, they would have a good chance of guessing correctly.

If they can reason through the problem a bit more, however, students may still be able to deduce the correct answer. Ask them to think about the size of an elephant. If a grown man stood next to an elephant, would he reach the elephant's back or head? No. Elephants, then, are definitely taller than 7 or 8 feet. Their legs are bigger in circumference than most men's bodies. Two thousand pounds is about what 10 large men would weigh altogether. Is an elephant bigger and heavier than 10 men? Yes, so the answer is D.

Point out to students that even though they did not actually know the weight of an adult male elephant, they were able to make a good guess by eliminating obviously wrong answers. This kind of reasoning can be applied to many standardized test questions with excellent results.

Coaching Clue — To try this as an exercise with students, tailor the steps outlined above to address a sample problem from one of your state's practice tests.

Critical Words and POE

As they apply the steps of POE, advise students to look for any critical (or extreme) words in the questions or answer choices. These words, which are often underlined, italicized, bold-faced, or set in all caps, may help students narrow down their choices or guide them in the right direction. Have them circle or underline any extreme words, such as:

NEVER	ONLY	ANY
EXCEPT	BEST	ALL
ALWAYS	NOT	NONE

Explain how these words can help students eliminate answer choices when common sense and prior experience are not helping. Very often, though not always, answer choices with critical or extreme words in them are wrong. If a student is forced to guess, you can advise her to cross out choices that involve these types of words.

Flip a Coin

If a student has narrowed down the answer options as much as possible by eliminating wrong or unlikely choices, but he still has two or three possible answers, he should just pick an answer—guess and move on. The odds are that over the course of the test he will guess correctly at least some of the time, thus improving his score. However, completely random guessing should be discouraged. It gives students the feeling that they can just give up and guess on hard questions when, in fact, a little POE and deductive reasoning could help them get close to the right answers. The fact is, unless there is a guessing penalty on your state's test, students have nothing to lose by guessing. Tell them to answer every question but to guess blindly only if they have exhausted all of their smart guessing strategies.

Reading Strategies

This section describes several helpful strategies students can use when facing questions on a reading test. Teach your students these helpful hints in order to build their testing confidence.

Reading for a Purpose

Explain to students that before they read anything, it is important to determine why they are reading it. For example, are they reading to get information, to be entertained, to learn something, or to explore another side of an issue? When students look at a text, they may not consciously think about why they are going to read it, beyond the fact that it is something they *have* to read. To ensure greater comprehension and better results when having to answer questions about a text, tell students to keep a purpose in mind when reading.

Questions, Questions

If students are familiar with the different types of questions they may encounter on a test, they will likely be better able to answer them. Review and explain the most familiar types of questions well in advance of the real tests. Reading questions can generally be organized into three categories: Instant Recall, Pause and Look, and Reader and Passage.

Instant Recall — This type of question asks students to recall information directly from the text, usually in a specific place. Example: "What color was Jennifer's balloon?"

Pause and Look — This type of question asks students to pause after reading, think back on what they read, and look for related information in the passage. The answer may not be found in one specific place in the text, but rather in a combination of details. Example: "How are the king and servant different?"

Reader and Passage — This type of question asks students to apply what they already know to what they have just read in the passage. Reader and Passage questions are the most challenging because they involve higher-level thinking skills, such as making inferences, drawing conclusions, or making comparisons. Example: "How did Jake feel when his dog was stolen?"

Coaching Clue — Using your state's practice tests, have the class brainstorm the types of questions that could be asked on your state's standardized reading test. Then, organize the questions by type in a chart for student reference.

After students are familiar with the different types of questions, prompt them to offer potential questions to ask after reading a text in class. Ask them what kinds of questions a test writer might ask about what they just read.

Using Graphic Organizers

Many reading tests ask students to complete graphic organizers with information from a text. The types of organizers are similar to those used to help students organize their ideas before writing. Some of the most common types of organizers students may be asked to complete include:

- ✗ Venn diagrams or compare/contrast charts
- ✗ Clustering organizers like webs or brainstorming charts
- ✗ Sequence maps or chain-of-events flowcharts
- ✗ Story maps

One of the best ways to prepare students for dealing with graphic organizers is to use them frequently in class, interchanging the types used with a variety of text structures. For example, a cluster or webbing diagram could be used for a nonfiction passage on dolphins, as well as to show the attributes or choices of a character from a folktale. When reading stories in class, have students compare two characters by completing a Venn diagram or a compare/contrast chart.

Identifying Text Structures

Students can also use text structure to help them find answers to questions. If students understand how a text is organized, they can focus on looking in a particular part of the text to answer each question most efficiently. For example, the basic structure of a story includes a beginning, a middle, and an end. The setting, characters, and other essential details are usually introduced to the reader at the beginning of a story. If a question following the passage asks for the name of a character or where the story takes place, students should know (based on the text's structure) to look for clues in the beginning of the story. If, on the other hand, there is a question about a problem or conflict, students should know that the details will probably be found somewhere in the middle of the story.

Coaching Clue — Read and discuss a variety of different text structures in class. Then, have students work in groups to write questions related to specific sections of a text. Have the groups exchange questions, then explain where in the passage each answer would most likely be found.

Modified SQ3R

Most teachers know SQ3R as an effective technique for retaining and comprehending reading material, but it can also be applied to test taking. Students can use an adaptation of this method when dealing with reading selections on standardized tests. This modified strategy can also be used with chapter books, textbooks, and expository texts, as well as short stories and other narrative passages.

Teach students to apply this modified version of SQ3R when approaching a reading selection and related questions on a test: Skim, Question, Read, Respond, and Review. By following these simple steps, students can tackle reading tests confidently and efficiently.

SKIM the passage before reading:

X   Look at the title. What does it tell you about the selection?

X   Look at any illustrations, photographs, charts, graphs, or maps.

X   Read through and label the types of questions before reading the passage.

QUESTION while skimming:

X   Turn the title into a question to make the subject more interesting. For example, if the title is "An Ancient Disk's Secret Message," change it into a question to focus your reading: "What is the ancient disk's secret message?"

X   Think about what you already know about specific words in the title or the subject of the passage. Try to connect your own knowledge and experience with the text you will be reading.

READ the passage actively:

X   Read with a purpose. Based on the title and other clues gleaned from skimming the passage, why are you going to read it? Why did the author write it in the first place? Was it to inform, entertain, persuade, or express?

X   Read carefully and at a comfortable pace, thinking about the questions, what you already know about the subject, and any new information you discover.

X   Mark up the text. As you read, underline words or phrases that stand out, make you think, or relate to one of the questions. Circle words you don't know or think might be important. Write any comments or questions you might have in the margins of the text.

RESPOND and REVIEW:

X   Read through the questions, answering the easiest ones first. If you are unsure about any questions, apply the X-O strategy.

X   Circle or underline any critical or extreme words in the questions and answer choices. Paraphrase each question by saying to yourself, "I'm actually looking for . . ."

X   Use the process of elimination to eliminate any answer choices you know are wrong. Cross these out and reread the remaining choices. Try to narrow it down to two choices for each question.

X   Make an educated guess between the two answer choices that remain. If necessary, reread the passage for any clues or ideas about the answer.

Coaching Clue — Use the *Modified SQ3R* reproducible (page 49) as a reference when discussing this strategy with your students.

Writing Strategies

Some states have writing tests at all grade levels while others test alternating grades (grades 6 and 8 or grades 5 and 7, for example). Check with your state's education department or agency to determine if your sixth graders will be asked to take a writing test.

Knowing How to Respond

One key strategy in writing an effective response to a prompt is determining what type of response to write. Although this may seem pretty straightforward, it is crucial that students understand the various writing terms and their meanings as they plan their responses.

Coaching Clue — Use the *Chart of Writing Terms* reproducible (page 50) to review the key descriptors your students may see in writing prompts at the sixth-grade level.

Using Graphic Organizers

Using graphic organizers is a great way for students to organize their thoughts during the prewriting process. Give students plenty of opportunities to use these organizers when writing in class. Some graphic organizers that are useful for the types of writing prompts students may encounter on standardized tests include:

- ✗ KWL charts
- ✗ Venn diagrams or compare/contrast charts
- ✗ Clustering organizers like webs or brainstorming charts
- ✗ Sequence maps or chain-of-events flowcharts
- ✗ Story maps

ROW Strategy

Preparing students for writing portions of standardized tests means preparing them to express their thoughts in written form. To help them think before they write, have students follow the ROW strategy: Read/Rephrase, Organize, and Write.

Read/Rephrase — Read the prompt, circling or underlining any key words and phrases, such as *describe*, *compare and contrast*, *explain*, or *support*. Rephrase the prompt to make it clearer or easier to understand. Think of the purpose for writing and what format to use.

Organize — Use a graphic organizer to collect your thoughts before writing. Pull specific details or quotations from the text and think of examples from your own experiences to back up your points. Record this information on the organizer.

Write — Using the graphic organizer as a guide, write your response or essay.

Math Strategies

Many of the questions on standardized math tests are word problems. In addition to using the general hints and strategies in this book, students can use the following approaches to tackle these tough opponents.

Draw It Out

Word problems often contain lots of details that can clutter students' minds when trying to solve them. The Draw It Out strategy helps visual learners solve word problems by having them draw or sketch out parts of problems in order to focus their thinking. By looking carefully at the wording of a problem and translating the words into pictures or symbols, students can often get a better handle on what the problem is actually asking them to find.

RIDDOTS Strategy

When students have difficulty solving word problems, encourage them to follow the steps outlined in the RIDDOTS strategy. This straightforward strategy can be modeled with a variety of word problems students may see on standardized tests. RIDDOTS is an acronym for the following process:

Read the entire problem carefully.
IDentify any key words that will help you solve the problem.
Determine what you need to find out. (What is the problem asking for?)
Omit unnecessary details.
Translate the words into an equation.
Solve the problem and choose an answer.

> ***Coaching Clue*** — Use the *RIDDOTS Strategy* reproducible (page 51) to guide students through an example and help them better understand how to use this strategy.
>
> To help students identify key words as in step 2, make a transparency of the *Math Vocabulary Chart* reproducible (page 52). In the additional space on the chart, have students add new words they find in word problems that indicate particular operations.

Top Five Things to Remember

Offer students these five tips to remember before, during, and after a test.

1. **Be confident!**
   Remember that you are prepped to do well. You have been "working out" to get ready for the test and can succeed. It's time to show what you can do.

2. **Be prepared!**
   Get a good night's sleep, eat a hearty breakfast, and wear clothes suitable for the test. Bring all of the materials you will need, such as pencils, a dictionary, or a calculator.

3. **Review the test before you begin.**
   Before you start, spend a few minutes reviewing the test carefully. Familiarize yourself with each section and then decide how to pace yourself.

4. **Be focused and relaxed.**
   Use the test-taking strategies you have learned to keep up your concentration. If you start to feel tense, take a few deep breaths and do some stretches to relax.

5. **Look over the test when you are finished.**
   Make sure you have not skipped any sections and that you have answered every question. Check your answer sheet to make sure the bubbles are filled in neatly and correctly. Proofread any writing for proper spelling, grammar, and punctuation.

Testing Questionnaire

Directions: Read each statement. Mark your answer by checking the appropriate box.

ALWAYS	SOME OF THE TIME	NEVER		
☐	☐	☐	1.	When I take a test, I feel confident that I am prepared and will do well.
☐	☐	☐	2.	The night before a test, I get a good night's sleep.
☐	☐	☐	3.	The morning before a test, I eat a good breakfast.
☐	☐	☐	4.	My mind wanders when I'm taking a test.
☐	☐	☐	5.	During a test, I forget what I have learned and then remember it after the test is over.
☐	☐	☐	6.	I make careless mistakes when taking a test.
☐	☐	☐	7.	I check my work and my answers before I turn in a test.
☐	☐	☐	8.	I rush to finish when I take a test.
☐	☐	☐	9.	When taking a test, I think too much about the questions, change my answers a lot, or don't answer at all.
☐	☐	☐	10.	If I don't know an answer, I narrow down my choices and guess.
☐	☐	☐	11.	If I don't know an answer, I skip the question and come back to it later.
☐	☐	☐	12.	During a test, my breathing gets weird or my body feels tense.
☐	☐	☐	13.	If I don't understand a question or what I'm supposed to do on a test, I ask for help.
☐	☐	☐	14.	If I start to lose concentration or get tired, I take a little break.

Directions: Discuss your answers for numbers 1–14 with the rest of the class. Then, read each statement below. Mark your answer by checking the box for TRUE or FALSE.

☐ TRUE ☐ FALSE 15. It is better to guess on a question than to leave it blank.

☐ TRUE ☐ FALSE 16. Being first to finish a test is better than being last.

☐ TRUE ☐ FALSE 17. If you get bored or can't concentrate, you should just put your head down and go to sleep.

☐ TRUE ☐ FALSE 18. It's a waste of time to check your work before turning in a test.

☐ TRUE ☐ FALSE 19. You should never take a break from a test.

☐ TRUE ☐ FALSE 20. It's important to relax and stay focused when taking a test.

Take a Good Look

Directions: Use the questions below to review the format, content, language, and style of your state's tests. Discuss the answers with your group. Be prepared to share with the rest of the class.

Reading Test
☐ What are the general directions given in the test booklet?

☐ What key words are used in the directions? Do you understand these directions?

☐ Is there room to write, make notes, or underline words in the test booklet?

☐ How many reading passages are there?

☐ How long is each passage?

☐ How are the passages organized on the pages?

☐ What kinds of passages are on the test? (stories, poems, excerpts from books, flyers, etc.)

☐ Are there any photographs, illustrations, charts, graphs, or maps?

☐ Do you know what italicized and boldfaced words are? Do they appear in the passages?

☐ What are the passages about?

☐ How many questions follow each passage?

☐ What types of questions are there? (multiple choice, short answer, essay, etc.)

☐ The first part of a multiple-choice question is called the stem. Are there any critical words in the stems of the questions, such as BEST, NOT, or EXCEPT?

☐ What items do you need to bring with you to the test? (scratch paper, pencils, etc.)

Math Test
☐ What general directions are given for the math test? Do you understand these directions?

☐ Are there specific directions for how to use the answer sheet or when to use a calculator?

☐ Is there a mathematics reference sheet or chart included in the test booklet? Where in the booklet is it located?

☐ What kinds of tools are you allowed to use? (calculator, ruler, etc.)

☐ What types of responses are required? (multiple choice, short answer, graphing, etc.)

☐ Is there space within the test booklet to work through problems?

☐ What types of problems are there? (computation, measurement, etc.)

☐ How many problems are there in all?

☐ What types of charts, pictures, or drawings are included? How do these graphics relate to the problems?

☐ What items do you need to bring with you to the test? (scratch paper, pencils, etc.)

X-O Strategy

Directions: Use the X-O strategy to guide you through the test-taking process. Be sure to mark your test as instructed below and to complete all portions of this handout.

Round 1: Read through the questions or problems on the test. As you read, answer all of the questions you can without too much effort or time. Mark those answers on your answer sheet.

    A.   Mark an X by each question that you think you can answer but are not sure about. Record the number of questions marked with an X here: _____

    B.   Mark an O by each question for which you would have to guess the answer. Record the number of questions marked with an O here: _____

Round 2: Go back through the test and try to answer all of the questions marked with an X.

    A.   If you need to, reread or review the questions. Look for additional information to help you clarify anything or support the answers you think are correct.

    B.   Mark the answers on your answer sheet.

Round 3: Go back through the test and try to answer all of the questions marked with an O.

    A.   Note any critical words in the questions. Circle or underline these words and write them on the following lines.

_____

_____

    B.   Apply POE, or the process of elimination.

        • Use common sense and logical reasoning to eliminate bad or unlikely answer choices. Think about how any critical words can help you determine the answers by eliminating some of the answer choices.

        • Cross out any answer choices that you know are incorrect or unlikely.

        • Try to narrow down the answer choices to two per question.

    C.   Use your own prior knowledge, information from the questions, or any other clues given (such as graphs or illustrations) to make educated guesses. Mark your answers on your answer sheet.

Modified SQ3R

SKIM – QUESTION – READ – RESPOND – REVIEW	
SKIM **before reading**	• Look at the title, headings, and subheadings. • Look at any pictures, charts, graphs, or maps. • Skim the questions to see what they are asking.
QUESTION **while skimming**	• Turn the title, headings, and subheadings into questions. • Think about what you already know about the subject. • Write down questions you have in the margins of the text or on a sheet of scratch paper.
READ the **passage actively**	• Read with a purpose. Think about the author's purpose for writing: to inform, entertain, express, or persuade. • Read the captions under any illustrations or graphics. • Mark any <u>underlined</u>, *italicized*, or **bold** words and phrases. • Make notes and underline words, phrases, or sentences that relate to the questions. • Stop and reread any unclear or confusing paragraphs. • Try to get a sense of the main idea of each paragraph and of the passage as a whole.
RESPOND **and REVIEW**	• Answer questions based on what you read. • Reread where necessary. • Use strategies to help you answer the questions.

Chart of Writing Terms

This chart lists terms that are frequently used in sixth-grade writing prompts.

Writing Term	Definition — What It Means
Compare	Take a close look at two or more things, characters, events, or ideas. Explain what is ALIKE about them.
Contrast	Take a close look at two or more things, characters, events, or ideas. Explain what is DIFFERENT about them.
Describe	Show rather than tell by painting a picture with words. Create a clear impression of a person, place, object, or event. Include details that relate to all five senses.
Explain	Give the who, what, when, where, why, and how about something. Provide details to make it easily understood.
Narrate (Write a Story)	Use story elements, such as setting, characters, and plot. The plot should have a beginning (introduction), a middle (problems/events), and an end (resolution/conclusion). Include details and literary elements to make the story interesting, and relate it to the prompt.
Persuade	State your view or opinion on a topic. Support your view with examples or reasons from the text or from your own experiences.
Reflect	Look back at or consider an event or idea from the text. Think deeply about the meaning of what you have read, relating it to your own experiences.

RIDDOTS Strategy

Write a word problem in this space:

Now, follow the steps in the left column to complete the boxes in the right column.

Read the entire problem carefully.	
IDentify any key words in the problem and write them in the box to the right.	
Determine what you need to find out: What are you trying to solve? What are you looking for?	
Omit unnecessary details from the word problem.	*Draw lines through words in the problem above that are NOT related to what you need to know or find out.*
Translate the words of the problem into an equation, formula, or mathematical expression.	
Solve the problem. • Show your work. (Use the back of this sheet if needed.) • Choose an answer, if provided. • Write your answer in the box to the right.	

Math Vocabulary Chart

This chart shows what different words can mean in story problems. In the extra space in each box, add other key math words that you find.

Meaning	Words and Phrases That Indicate Mathematical Operations		
Add	increased by	more than	total of
	added to	sum	combined
	altogether		
Subtract	decreased by	minus	less
	fewer than	less than	difference between/of
Multiply	times	multiplied by	increased by a factor of
	product of		
Divide	per	out of	percent (divide by 100)
	ratio of	quotient of	
Equals	is/are	was/were	is equal to
	will be	gives	is the same as
	yields	sold for	

Skill-Building Reading Activities

This chapter includes 11 different activities designed to help you build and reinforce students' reading comprehension skills. Each activity provides an engaging way for students to practice one or more key skills that will be assessed on your state's standardized tests. Students will be asked to use their knowledge, experiences, and imaginations. Each activity is structured in the following format:

✗ Skills/State Standards—breakdown of the skills addressed in the activity

✗ Description—brief summary of the activity

✗ Materials You Need—list of materials required for the activity

✗ Getting Ready—tips for the teacher and a description of what to do in order to prepare for the activity

✗ Introducing the Activity—suggestions for introducing the activity and capturing students' interest

✗ Modeling the Activity—ideas for demonstrating the activity (if applicable)

✗ Activity in Practice—step-by-step instructions for working through the activity

✗ Extensions—variations, extensions, and other teaching suggestions

The activities in this chapter are designed to be hands-on and group-oriented, requiring active participation by your students. However, they are also flexible in nature and can be modified to meet your students' needs, as well as give students individual practice. You can use the activities in any order. You may find that some are more suited to the particular needs of your students than others.

Some activities also include reproducible pages. These pages are found at the end of this chapter, beginning on page 78.

The matrix on pages 54 and 55 organizes the activities by the predominant skills or standards they address. Some activities address more than one skill and may, therefore, appear under more than one category on the chart.

Matrix of Skills Addressed in Reading Activities

Skill/State Standard	Activity	Page
Using root words, prefixes, and suffixes	Word Hunt	62
Identifying connotations, analogies, and multiple-meaning words	What Does It All Mean? Word Hunt	60 62
Using context clues	What Does It All Mean? Word Hunt	60 62
Identifying main idea and supporting details	Theme Team Mainly So	72 74
Paraphrasing and summarizing	Plot, Plot, Plot Mainly So	58 74
Analyzing character	Character Mingle and Mix How It Looks to Me Tone It Up	56 68 76
Understanding setting	Character Mingle and Mix Dark and Stormy Night	56 70
Analyzing plot, conflict, and problem resolution	Plot, Plot, Plot Dark and Stormy Night	58 70
Recognizing theme	Theme Team	72
Understanding foreshadowing and flashback	What Lies Ahead?	64
Understanding figurative language and symbolism	What Does It All Mean?	60
Understanding point of view	Character Mingle and Mix How It Looks to Me	56 68
Recognizing style, tone, and mood	What Does It All Mean? Word Hunt Dark and Stormy Night Tone It Up	60 62 70 76
Identifying the author's purpose	Fact Finders Mainly So	66 74

Matrix of Skills [continued]

Skill/State Standard	Activity	Page
Understanding cause and effect	Plot, Plot, Plot	58
Distinguishing fact from opinion	Fact Finders	66
Comparing and contrasting	Character Mingle and Mix	56
	What Lies Ahead?	64
	How It Looks to Me	68
	Theme Team	72
Making inferences, drawing conclusions, and making generalizations	What Lies Ahead?	64
	Theme Team	72
	Mainly So	74
Making predictions	What Lies Ahead?	64
Supporting ideas with evidence and experience	What Lies Ahead?	64
	Theme Team	72
Using outlines, time lines, and graphic organizers	Plot, Plot, Plot	58
	Theme Team	72
	Mainly So	74
Analyzing text structures and organizational patterns	Plot, Plot, Plot	58

Character Mingle and Mix

Description

In this activity, students will work in teams to make posters showing characters from different stories interacting. Before they draw or paint their posters, they will first answer questions about the characters' motivations, conflicts, points of view, and changes they undergo. After analyzing the characters, students will work with their teams to discuss how these characters would interact if they met. As students discuss their chosen characters, they will compare and contrast their traits. Students will also work together to come up with interesting settings in which their characters might meet. Students will then present their posters to the class, describing what they think would happen if their chosen characters ever met each other.

> ### Skills/State Standards
> X Analyzing character
> X Comparing and contrasting
> X Understanding setting
> X Understanding point of view

Materials You Need

- *Character Mingle and Mix* reproducible (page 78)
- Poster board or newsprint
- Colored pencils, markers, crayons, paints, or other art supplies
- Overhead projector and supplies

Getting Ready

For this activity, students should choose characters from books, plays, or stories they have recently read on their own. If you anticipate that students will have trouble selecting characters, have them read specific stories prior to the activity and assign them characters from those texts.

Make student handouts using the *Character Mingle and Mix* reproducible. Make an additional copy on a transparency to use during the modeling portion of the activity.

Introducing the Activity

Ask students to think of a favorite character from a story, play, or book they have recently read. Tell them that when they analyze character, they should think about a character's traits, motivations, conflicts (internal and external), points of view, relationships with others, and changes they experience. Discuss these aspects of character and clarify any questions students may have about character analysis. Then, tell students that in this activity they will be drawing or painting posters that show their favorite characters interacting.

Modeling the Activity

Show students how to complete the *Character Mingle and Mix* handout using your transparency and an overhead projector. Choose a character that is familiar to the class and complete the handout, explaining the terms and answering questions as you go.

Activity in Practice

1. Divide the class into teams of three or four students.

2. Tell students that they will each pick a character to analyze. Make sure that each student on a team chooses a different character. If two students on one team choose the same character, have one of them switch to another team.

3. Give each student a copy of the *Character Mingle and Mix* handout.

4. Have students write the titles and authors of their books or stories and answer the questions about their chosen characters. Help them answer these questions if necessary.

5. After they have completed the handouts, instruct each team to discuss what might happen if their characters met. You might want to write the following questions on the board: How would the characters react to each other? Which character would be the friendliest? Which would be the most timid or most aggressive? Which characters would get along the best and why? Encourage students to use their imaginations while thinking about and discussing these scenarios.

6. Have students on each team decide on a place where their characters could meet. Again, encourage students to be creative. They could have the characters meet in a contemporary setting, such as a school cafeteria or movie theater, or in an older setting like a castle. Tell them to decide what each character would be doing when they all meet.

7. Give students art supplies and poster board or newsprint, and ask them to create their posters. All team members should participate in making the posters.

8. Have teams present their finished posters to the class. Tell them to explain what they drew and to answer any questions that other students may have about the characters.

9. Display the posters in the classroom.

Extensions

To simplify the activity, you could have students work in pairs to make posters showing how two characters would interact. You could also modify the activity by having students make murals instead of posters.

The *Character Mingle and Mix* handout can be used anytime you want to have students practice analyzing character.

Plot, Plot, Plot

Description

In this activity, students will work in teams to make time lines showing the order of events in a reading selection. Given slips of paper with descriptions of eight events from the selection, each team will first determine the correct order of events. Then, each team will use the *Plot, Plot, Plot* handout to make a time line showing the events in the proper order.

Using the handout, students will answer questions about the main conflict and problem resolution in the reading selection (if appropriate). They will also discuss the selection's organizational pattern (cause/effect, compare/contrast, chronological, etc.). This activity can be used with either narrative or expository works.

Materials You Need

- *Plot, Plot, Plot* reproducible (page 79)
- Scissors (for you)

Getting Ready

Choose a short story, play, or nonfiction piece for students to read. The reading selection should include at least eight distinct events. You may want to choose a piece based on what you want students to practice most in this activity. For example, if you want students to work on identifying conflict and problem resolution, choose a story in which there is a clear conflict and resolution.

Once you have chosen a reading selection, write one-sentence descriptions of eight separate events from the selection. Make six copies of this events sheet. Cut each sheet into eight strips—each strip listing a different event—so that you have six sets of events.

Make student handouts using the *Plot, Plot, Plot* reproducible.

Introducing the Activity

Tell students that they will be working on several important skills in this activity, including sequencing; analyzing plot, conflict, and problem resolution; and making time lines. Discuss why knowing the sequence of events is important and how sequence can affect a story or nonfiction piece.

You may also want to review time lines with the class, showing them examples from a social studies or science text. Point out how time lines organize information, making it easier for the reader to comprehend a selection.

Activity in Practice

1. Divide the class into six teams. Give each student a copy of the reading selection. Allow enough time for students to read the piece independently.

2. Distribute one set of events and a *Plot, Plot, Plot* handout to each team. Tell students to read the slips of paper that describe different events from the selection.

3. Instruct students to work together to figure out the proper order of events. They can reread the piece to check the order. When they have decided on the correct order, each team should complete the time line on the handout. Have them list events in chronological order, with Event 1 being the earliest event. Show them how to make the time line if necessary.

4. After students complete the time line, have them discuss and answer the questions on the handout. If relevant to the selection, have them discuss which events involved the main conflict and resolution.

5. Help students determine what the selection's organizational pattern is. If necessary, review the types of patterns with the class: cause/effect, compare/contrast, inductive, deductive, chronological, etc.

6. Answer any questions students may have about the activity.

Extensions

For practice with summarizing, have teams retell or act out the story or events from the reading selection. (Have students prepare by referring to their completed handouts.) For practice with analyzing cause and effect, ask teams to discuss how certain events on the time line caused other events to happen. Do most of the events cause other events to occur?

Extend the activity by challenging students to make outlines or other graphic organizers of the events you gave them. If you wish to modify the activity, partially fill in the time line, outline, or other graphic organizer, and then have students complete it.

What Does It All Mean?

Description

In this activity, students will work in teams to identify the connotations and other meanings of words in context. Each team will receive a one-page excerpt from a narrative selection that contains several underlined vocabulary words. Students will discuss and identify each word's connotations, drawing on context and their own prior experiences. They will also come up with other meanings for each word and discuss how these words and their connotations contribute to the excerpt's style and mood. Students will then consult dictionaries and thesauruses to check their answers.

> ### Skills/State Standards
> ✗ Identifying connotations, analogies, and multiple-meaning words
> ✗ Using context clues
> ✗ Recognizing style, tone, and mood
> ✗ Understanding figurative language and symbolism

This activity will give students practice with a variety of word-identification strategies and help them focus on the emotional impact of words. The *What Does It All Mean?* handout will guide students through the activity and give them a place to record their answers.

Materials You Need
- *What Does It All Mean?* reproducible (page 80)
- Dictionaries
- Thesauruses
- Overhead projector and supplies

Getting Ready

Select a one-page reading selection to use for the activity. The selection should contain about five or six words that have strong connotations. You may want to consider using an excerpt from a mystery novel or other text in which words have strong connotations that contribute to the work's overall mood and style. Key in or photocopy the selection, and underline the vocabulary words students will be asked to identify.

Gather enough dictionaries and thesauruses so that you have one of each available for each team of students to use.

Make student handouts using the *What Does It All Mean?* reproducible. Then, make an additional copy on a transparency to use during the modeling portion of the activity.

Introducing the Activity

Review the concept of connotations with students. Be sure they understand the difference between a word's connotations and its denotations. Discuss how connotations or the emotional impact of a word contributes to a text's mood and style. Also, remind students that many words have more than one meaning. Review how to use a dictionary and a thesaurus if necessary. Tell the class that in this activity they will work in teams to identify connotations and multiple meanings of words.

Modeling the Activity

Show students how to complete a row of the *What Does It All Mean?* handout using your transparency and an overhead projector. Write an example word in a sentence in the first column, then describe the word's connotations. You may want to think aloud as you do this to model what connotations are. Then, write alternate meanings of the word. Answer any questions students may have so far about the activity.

Activity in Practice

1. Divide the class into teams of three to five students. Distribute copies of the reading selection and the *What Does It All Mean?* handout.

2. Ask students to discuss the connotations of each underlined word with their teams. Remind them that connotations are the feelings a word evokes. There are no exact answers. Students should list all of the connotations discussed in their teams.

3. Next, have students list alternate meanings for each word. Instruct them to use dictionaries and thesauruses to check their answers.

4. Have each team discuss the overall mood of the passage. How do the words' connotations contribute to the excerpt's tone or mood?

5. Ask students how word choice contributes to the author's style. How would they describe the author's writing style?

6. Have teams share their results with the rest of the class.

Extensions

To extend the activity, have students write analogies, metaphors, or similes using the new vocabulary words. This will help students retain the words' meanings. You can also have students write short stories that each incorporate three or more of the words.

The *What Does It All Mean?* handout can be used repeatedly to give students practice with connotations and multiple-meaning words.

Word Hunt

Description

In this competitive game activity, students will practice using root words, prefixes, and suffixes as a strategy for identifying words. After dividing the class into teams, you will write root words, prefixes, and suffixes on the board, and provide each team with a reading selection featuring words that contain those affixes and roots. Each team will then compete to complete the *Word Hunt* handout, which requires them to find words that use each of the roots, prefixes, and suffixes you listed. After finding the words, students will use context clues, prior knowledge, or dictionaries to figure out the meaning of each word. The team that finishes first wins.

After the game is finished, the class will discuss the connotations of each word and how word choice contributes to the selection's tone. This activity can be used with any kind of text.

Skills/State Standards

X Using root words, prefixes, and suffixes

X Using context clues

X Identifying connotations, analogies, and multiple-meaning words

X Recognizing style, tone, and mood

Materials You Need

- *Word Hunt* reproducible (page 81)
- Dictionaries

Getting Ready

Choose a reading selection to use with the activity. Make a list of 10 affixes and root words that appear in vocabulary of the text.

Make student handouts using the *Word Hunt* reproducible.

Introducing the Activity

If necessary, review how to use a dictionary. Remind students that a dictionary can be used to find the meanings of root words, as well as prefixes and suffixes. Explain these word parts to students and remind them that knowing word parts can help them figure out the meanings of unfamiliar words. It may be helpful to review the meanings of some common affixes, such as *un-*, *pre-*, *post-*, *-ly*, *-ed*, and *–ment*.

Tell students that in this activity they will compete as teams to find words that use certain affixes and roots.

Modeling the Activity

Show students how to look up words in a dictionary. You may want to show them a sample entry and how to read each part of the entry. Point out how the roots of words are often given in each entry and how prefixes and suffixes can be looked up separately. Then, review how words can be broken down into affixes and roots. Write several examples of such words on the board.

Activity in Practice

1. Divide the class into teams of five or six students.

2. Distribute copies of the reading selection, the *Word Hunt* handout, and a dictionary to each team.

3. Tell students that you are about to give them a list of affixes and roots that appear in words in the reading selection. After they have the list, students will write each root word, prefix, or suffix in the first column of their handouts. In the second column, they will write a word from the selection that uses each root or affix. In the last column, they will write the meaning of the word. They can use prior knowledge, context, or a dictionary to find the meaning of each word.

4. Tell students that the first team to complete the handout wins. You may want to offer a prize to the winning team.

5. Answer any questions students have, then write the list of 10 affixes and root words on the board. Tell teams to start hunting.

6. After each team has completed the handout and the game has been won, have the class discuss the connotations of the various words they found. Ask students to describe how the words they found contributed to the overall tone of the reading selection.

7. Answer any questions students may have about the activity. Remind them that by knowing and identifying root words, prefixes, and suffixes, they can often decipher the meanings of new words, thereby increasing their vocabulary.

Extensions

You can extend the activity by having teams come up with other words that use the same roots, prefixes, and suffixes as the words you provided for the activity. This will help reinforce the meanings of these word parts.

You can also have students write analogies using these words, or challenge them further to write poems, articles, or stories using all 10 of the words.

What Lies Ahead?

Description

In this activity, students will practice interpreting foreshadowing in a literary passage and make predictions about what happens next in the story. Drawing on their own experiences, knowledge of literary devices, and the text itself, they will make inferences and draw conclusions. Then, they will work in teams to write possible outcomes of the story, supporting their predictions with textual evidence and personal experience. After they hear the actual conclusion of the story, students will discuss how their own versions compared with the original story.

Skills/State Standards

✗ Understanding foreshadowing and flashback

✗ Making inferences, drawing conclusions, and making generalizations

✗ Making predictions

✗ Comparing and contrasting

✗ Supporting ideas with evidence and experience

Materials You Need

• *What Lies Ahead?* reproducible (page 82)

Getting Ready

Find a story, play, or poem in which foreshadowing plays an important role. If possible, use a selection that is unfamiliar to the class.

Make student handouts using the *What Lies Ahead?* reproducible.

Introducing the Activity

Ask students to describe the concept of foreshadowing. Explain that when something is foreshadowed in a work, there is a sign or suggestion that something will happen later in the story. Read the following sentences to the class. Ask students what they think might happen next in each situation.

• Suddenly, the sky grew dark and gloomy. Thunderclouds gathered on the horizon.

• Johann smirked knowingly when no one else was looking.

• A pebble trickled down in front of Catherine. She ignored it and kept walking in the cave.

Ask students to think of other examples of foreshadowing in works they have read and clarify any questions students may have about this literary device. Tell students that they will be working in teams to predict what will happen next in a story based on a foreshadowing event.

Activity in Practice

1. Divide the class into small teams. Distribute copies of the *What Lies Ahead?* handout.

2. Read the story, play, or poem you have chosen aloud to the class. Stop at the point just after the foreshadowing event.

3. Have each team discuss and write down what the foreshadowing event is.

4. Next, ask students to brainstorm and discuss what might happen next. Have each team designate a scribe who will write a possible scene or conclusion to the story based on what the students on the team think will happen.

5. Instruct students to answer the question about why they think that particular scenario will happen. Encourage them to support their predictions with details from the text and their own experiences. Remind students that it is not important whether their predictions are right or wrong—simply making the predictions helps students think carefully about the text and understand it better.

6. Ask volunteers to read the teams' scenes/conclusions aloud to the class.

7. After all of the teams have shared their predictions, continue reading the rest of the story. When you are finished, discuss how the students' versions of the story compared and contrasted with the actual version. Then, have students decide how predictable the foreshadowing event was.

8. Answer any questions students may have about the activity.

Extensions

Extend the activity by having students discuss other literary devices, such as flashback. Ask them to describe examples of flashback they have seen used in stories they have read. Discuss whether the use of flashback is an effective device in those stories. To have students work on flashback specifically, ask them to write scenes that take place earlier than the action of the story you read them. For example, they could describe memories from a character's childhood.

Instead of reading part of a story, you could show students an illustration from a graphic novel or illustrated story and have them make predictions based solely on the illustration. Then, after students have made their predictions, read the text from the novel or story to see how accurate students' predictions were.

Fact Finders

Description

In this competitive game activity, students will work in teams to locate facts and opinions in advertisements and articles. The first team to find four facts and one opinion wins the round. As a class, students will discuss what makes each statement a fact or an opinion.

Skills/State Standards

X Distinguishing fact from opinion

X Identifying the author's purpose

Materials You Need

- *Fact Finders* reproducible (page 83)
- Magazines, newspapers, flyers, and other persuasive written materials
- Sample print advertisement
- Overhead projector and supplies

Getting Ready

Using an assortment of magazines, newspapers, and flyers, cut out several print ads and articles, including op-ed pieces and other texts meant to persuade the reader. Each ad or article that you select should contain a variety of statements, and at least four facts and one opinion each. (You can modify these numbers as you see fit.) Make copies of the ads and articles so that you have one set for each team of students. Choose another ad to present to the class as an example. Copy this onto a transparency if possible.

Make student handouts using the *Fact Finders* reproducible. Each team will need one copy of the handout for each ad or article that they will read. Make an additional copy on a transparency. Use the transparency during the modeling portion of the activity.

Introducing the Activity

Write the following statements on the board or on a transparency:

- The earth is 93 million miles away from the sun.

- The earth is a beautiful planet.

Ask students to tell you which statement is a fact and which is an opinion. Discuss what makes a statement a fact (it can be verified as true) or an opinion (it expresses someone's ideas, feelings, or thoughts about something).

Have students think of phrases that usually introduce opinions, such as "I think . . ." or "In my opinion . . ." Ask if they can think of any instances in which opinions would not start with phrases like these.

Explain that ads and persuasive articles usually include a mixture of facts and opinions in order to present convincing arguments. Discuss how the purpose of most ads is to persuade people to buy things. Tell students that in this activity they will practice determining whether statements that appear in ads and articles are facts or opinions.

Modeling the Activity

Show students the sample ad you selected. Ask if they can identify two facts and one opinion in the ad. Then, using your transparency of the *Fact Finders* handout, model how to fill in the handout. Discuss the purpose of the ad and whether it is effective. Ask students to explain their opinions.

Activity in Practice

1. Divide the class into teams of four students.
2. Give each team one set of ads and articles. Place the documents facedown. Then, distribute copies of the *Fact Finders* handout, giving each team one copy of the handout for each ad or article they will read.
3. Explain the rules of the game. Tell students that in each round, they will work with their team members to find four facts and one opinion in an ad or article. Then, they will identify the author's purpose. Students will use this information to complete the handout. When they are done, students should raise their hands. The first team to complete the handout successfully wins the round. Teams will use a separate handout for each ad or article they read.
4. Begin round one. Tell students to begin with the first ad or article. The round ends after all of the teams have completed their handouts.
5. Repeat the steps with the other selections. The team that wins the most rounds wins the game. Consider offering small prizes to the winners.
6. Answer any questions students may have about identifying facts and opinions.

Extensions

Modify the activity by having students complete it as a noncompetitive exercise. Simply have groups identify facts and opinions using the handout.

Have students use a combination of facts and opinions to create their own ads or write their own persuasive articles.

How It Looks to Me

Description

For this activity, you will assign every student on a team a different character from a story or play. Each student will answer questions about the character's point of view in a particular scene from the story, and then sketch the scene from that character's perspective. After completing the handouts, students on each team will compare and discuss their sketches and how each character's point of view differs or overlaps with the others'. This activity will give students practice analyzing point of view and understanding how it affects the way a story is told. This activity can also be used with poems or other literary works in which different points of view are represented.

Skills/State Standards

X Understanding point of view

X Analyzing character

X Comparing and contrasting

Materials You Need

- *How It Looks to Me* reproducible (page 84)
- Colored pencils and other drawing materials
- Overhead projector and supplies

Getting Ready

Choose a story, play, or other literary work to use for the activity. Your selection should be relatively short since you will be reading it aloud to the class. It should also involve at least three characters with differing points of view.

You will also want to select another text to use during the modeling portion of the activity. A simple fairy tale, such as "The Three Little Pigs," will work well.

Make student handouts using the *How It Looks to Me* reproducible. Then, make an additional copy on a transparency to use during the modeling portion of the activity.

Introducing the Activity

Tell students that they will be working with characters and point of view. Explain that the point of view they experience when reading or hearing a story depends on who is telling it. For example, in "The Three Little Pigs," each scene differs depending on whether the wolf or one of the little pigs is telling the story—and each little pig has his own idea of what's going on in any given scene. Tell students that in this activity, they will describe what is going on in a scene from different characters' points of view and then sketch the scene. Clarify any questions students may have about point of view before proceeding with the activity.

Modeling the Activity

Show students how to complete the handout using your *How It Looks to Me* transparency. Take the character of the wolf in "The Three Little Pigs" as an example and answer the questions. Here are some possible answers for questions 4–7:

4. *Three little pigs are building houses in the forest, intruding on my home and peaceful way of living.* 5. *I feel angry about them building on my property.* 6. *I want them to go away.*
7. *First, I'll blow down their little houses. Then, I'll chase the pigs away.*

You may also want to sketch a scene from the tale illustrating the wolf's point of view.

Activity in Practice

1. Divide the class into teams of four students.

2. Distribute copies of the *How It Looks to Me* handout, along with colored pencils and other drawing supplies.

3. Read the selection aloud to the class. Then, assign every student on each team a different character from the story or play. If there are fewer than four characters in the story, you may want to include an unusual "character," such as a tree or some other object. Having students illustrate the story from the point of view of an object will challenge them to be especially creative.

4. Have each team select a scene that includes all of their characters. Then, instruct students to complete the handout. Each student should present the scene from her particular character's point of view. Help students answer the questions if necessary. Encourage them to use their imaginations when thinking about their characters' points of view. How would it feel to be inside each character's head?

5. After students have made their sketches, have team members compare and contrast their answers and sketches. Ask them to discuss how different and similar each character's point of view was.

6. As a class, discuss how point of view affects the way a story is told.

Extension

You can extend the activity by having teams make four-part murals or posters based on their sketches, using tempera paints and long rolls of butcher paper.

Dark and Stormy Night

Description

In this activity, students will work in teams to rewrite a story by giving it a different setting. First, students will identify the tale's setting and how the setting contributes to the story's plot and mood. Then, students will rewrite the story, having it take place under very different circumstances. For example, if the story takes place in a city, students can rewrite it so that it takes place in the country or on a remote island. By rewriting the tale, students will be forced to think about how setting affects the plot and events in the story, as well as how setting contributes to the overall mood.

Skills/State Standards

✗ Understanding setting

✗ Analyzing plot, conflict, and problem resolution

✗ Recognizing style, tone, and mood

Materials You Need

- *Dark and Stormy Night* reproducible (page 85)
- Overhead projector and supplies (optional)

Getting Ready

Select a story (or stories) you want students to rewrite. You may choose to assign each team a different story or have the entire class work on the same story. (If you choose the latter, you could have students compare and contrast their new versions.)

Whatever you decide, be sure to select stories with easily identifiable settings that contribute significantly to the stories' plots and moods. Make copies of the stories for students.

Rewrite a scene from a story that is familiar to your students by altering the setting. Use this new version of the story to model the activity for students. Copy the story onto a transparency if desired.

Make student handouts using the *Dark and Stormy Night* reproducible.

Introducing the Activity

Tell students that in this activity they will be rewriting a story by changing the story's setting. Review setting and how it contributes to plot and mood. Remind students that setting refers to where and when a story takes place, and that setting can affect the events and characters. You may want to discuss stories they have read in class in which setting plays an important role.

Modeling the Activity

Share with students your version of a familiar story rewritten with a new setting. Use an overhead projector if desired or simply read the story aloud. Discuss the differences between your version of the story and the original tale. Ask students to describe how the new setting affects the characters and the plot.

Activity in Practice

1. Divide the class into teams of four students.

2. Distribute copies of the *Dark and Stormy Night* handout.

3. Assign a story to each team and have them read it together. You might want to have a volunteer from each team read the story aloud to the other members of the team.

4. Instruct each team to complete Part 1 of the handout together. They should discuss all aspects of setting. You might want to ask students to answer the following questions: Is the story set in the city or country? Does it take place at night or during the day? What are the weather conditions? Does the action occur in the past or is it taking place right now?

5. Ask teams to discuss how setting helps establish the mood of each story. For example, a dark and stormy nighttime setting may create a mood of gloom and danger.

6. Next, have each team rewrite their story by changing the setting in some significant way. Tell students to use their imaginations as they consider how to change the setting. They might want to have the story take place in a city, on a remote island, in a medieval castle, in ancient Egypt, or on a farm. They could introduce a severe weather condition, such as a blizzard or hurricane, or have the story take place at a different time of day or during a different year.

7. Have students think about and discuss how changing the setting would change the events of the story, as well as the mood. What kind of mood do students want to create?

8. Each team should brainstorm what they want to change in their story. A designated team scribe will write down the rewritten tale. Tell students that they should rewrite as many details as they want. If they run out of room on the handout, they can continue the story on the back of the sheet or on another sheet of paper.

9. After teams have written their stories, have volunteers read the new versions aloud.

10. As a class, discuss how changing setting can affect plot and mood. Point out that by changing setting, students changed many other elements of the story as well.

Extensions

You can modify the activity by giving each team specific instructions on how to change the setting. For example, you could tell a team to set the story in Chicago during the 1920s or on the fateful voyage of the *Titanic*.

To extend the activity, you could collect all of the stories and publish them in a class anthology.

Theme Team

Description

In this activity, students will work in teams to match themes with stories, poems, or plays they have read. After discussing which theme goes with which text, students will use the *Theme Team* handout to record their conclusions. Then, they will be asked to support their answers using their own experiences and evidence from the texts.

Completing the handout will give students practice using graphic organizers. As a class, students will also discuss which themes appear in more than one work, connecting themes across texts. Finally, by identifying themes in particular works, students will draw conclusions about the important messages in those texts.

Skills/State Standards

- ✗ Recognizing theme
- ✗ Using outlines, time lines, and graphic organizers
- ✗ Making inferences, drawing conclusions, and making generalizations
- ✗ Supporting ideas with evidence and experience
- ✗ Comparing and contrasting
- ✗ Identifying main idea and supporting details

Materials You Need

- *Theme Team* reproducible (page 86)
- Overhead projector and supplies

Getting Ready

This activity requires students to match themes with texts they have read. Choose at least five different texts that students have read recently and write down a major theme from each one. You may want to choose two or more texts that share common themes. You may also want to identify more than one theme for a particular text.

Make student handouts using the *Theme Team* reproducible. Then, make an additional copy on a transparency to use during the modeling portion of the activity.

Introducing the Activity

Tell students that they will be identifying themes in this activity. Review the concept of theme and remind students that themes can often be stated as messages or mottoes. "Without hard work, success is impossible" and "Minding your own business is the best policy" are just two examples of themes. Have the class brainstorm other common themes found throughout literature. Answer any questions students may have about theme.

Modeling the Activity

Show students how to complete the chart on the *Theme Team* handout if necessary. Using your transparency of the handout, write a short list of themes in the first column. Then, write the titles of well-known literary works that explore each theme in the second column.

Activity in Practice

1. Divide the class into five teams.

2. Give each team a copy of the *Theme Team* handout.

3. List five themes from five different texts on the board. The themes should be from texts that every student has read. In a second column, write the titles of the texts in which the themes are explored.

4. Instruct teams to complete their handouts by working together to match each theme with the corresponding text. Remind students that some themes may apply to more than one text.

5. Have teams discuss which themes, if any, relate to more than one work. Then, have each team present one theme and the work it matches. Ask students to say how that theme goes with that work, using evidence from the text or their own experiences.

6. After all of the teams have presented their findings, have the class discuss which themes were common to more than one text. This will give students practice with comparing and contrasting themes.

Extensions

To make the activity more challenging, give students many themes to choose from—some of which do not relate to any of the texts listed. Inform students that some themes do not go with any of the works and have them complete the activity.

You can extend the activity by having students brainstorm additional themes that are explored in each work listed.

You could modify the activity to have students match main ideas with various nonfiction selections. If you choose to focus on main idea, adapt the handout and your introduction to the activity accordingly.

Mainly So

Description

At the sixth-grade level, students are usually tested on identifying the main idea in specific paragraphs of narrative and expository texts. Students are also sometimes asked to identify the main idea of an entire article. The *Mainly So* handout can be used to help students identify the main idea and supporting details in both paragraphs and whole texts. As they determine the main idea, students will use critical-thinking and inferencing skills. The activity will also give students practice summarizing, identifying the author's purpose, and using graphic organizers.

Skills/State Standards

- ✗ Identifying main idea and supporting details
- ✗ Making inferences, drawing conclusions, and making generalizations
- ✗ Using outlines, time lines, and graphic organizers
- ✗ Identifying the author's purpose
- ✗ Paraphrasing and summarizing

Materials You Need

- *Mainly So* reproducible (page 87)
- Overhead projector and supplies

Getting Ready

Select an appropriate text to use for the activity. Although any variety of texts would work well, be sure to choose a text that includes paragraphs with clear main ideas and supporting details. A scientific essay would work especially well. When you have chosen a text, make copies for students as needed.

Make student handouts using the *Mainly So* reproducible. Make an additional copy of the handout on a transparency to use during the modeling portion of the activity.

Introducing the Activity

Review the concept of main idea with students. Explain that the main idea is the most important idea or message in a piece. It may or may not be clearly stated in the text. Tell students that a main idea is usually supported by details, such as examples or facts. These details help reinforce the main idea. Tell students that in this activity they will practice identifying the main idea and supporting details.

Modeling the Activity

1. Pass out copies of the text you want students to read. Instruct students to read the first paragraph.

2. Place your transparency of the *Mainly So* handout on an overhead projector. Ask students to describe the main focus of the paragraph they just read. Try to distill their responses into a single phrase or sentence. Write the main idea in the center of the graphic organizer.

3. Next, ask students to identify details or examples from the text that support the main idea. Write these in the other ovals of the web.

4. Answer any questions students may have about main idea and supporting details.

Activity in Practice

1. Divide the class into teams of four students.

2. Distribute copies of the *Mainly So* handout. Make sure that each team has several copies (four to six, depending on how many paragraphs there are in the reading selection).

3. Have students read the next paragraph of the text. Teams should discuss what the main idea and supporting details are and fill out their graphic organizers accordingly.

4. Have students repeat the activity, using additional copies of the handout for each paragraph, until they have read the entire text.

5. Remind students that identifying main idea is a challenging but important skill. If appropriate, have students use their handouts to identify the main idea of the whole text.

6. After students have completed the graphic organizers, have them state the author's purpose for writing the piece. Help them formulate this statement. Students might say something like, "The author's purpose was to write an article about how lichen changes the color of rock formations."

7. To conclude the activity, have students orally summarize paragraphs or the entire text. Have them refer to their completed handouts since they contain information about what the text is about along with the relevant details.

8. Answer any questions students may have about main idea, supporting details, summarizing, author's purpose, and graphic organizers.

Extensions

To modify the activity, fill in part of the handout before making copies for students. For example, you could fill in some of the supporting details and have students identify just the main idea or vice versa.

To extend the activity, ask students to paraphrase paragraphs from the text. Have them do this orally, paraphrasing main ideas and statements for other team members.

Tone It Up

Description

In this activity, students will work in teams to write imaginative letters to well-known characters. Each team will adopt a specific tone in writing their letter. Once their letters are complete, teams will trade letters with each other. Then, each team will try to identify the tone of the other team's letter. This activity gives students practice with creating and identifying authorial tone, as well as working with known characters.

Materials You Need

- *Tone It Up Cutouts* reproducible (page 88)
- *Tone It Up* reproducible (page 89)
- Scissors (for you)
- Overhead projector and supplies

Getting Ready

Make one copy of the *Tone It Up Cutouts* reproducible. If you wish, write additional characters and tones in the empty boxes. You may want to add characters from books that students have read recently, popular television characters, comic-strip heroes, or even famous people that are familiar to students. Once you have added all of the names and tones you wish to include, cut up your copy of the page. Save these strips of paper in two separate envelopes, one marked "Character" and the other marked "Tone." You will use these strips to assign each team a tone and character when you are ready to practice the activity.

Make student handouts using the *Tone It Up* reproducible. Then, make an additional copy of the handout on a transparency. Choose a tone and a favorite character, and write a sample letter on the transparency. Share this letter with students during the modeling portion of the activity.

Introducing the Activity

Discuss the concept of tone with your class. Tell students that an author creates a tone when his attitude toward the subject is reflected in the text. Tone affects the way a reader receives information about a subject. For example, an article about seashells that has an objective tone would be very different from a story about seashells that has a sentimental tone. Ask students to identify the tone in each of several works they have just read. Then, explain to students that in this activity they will be writing letters to familiar characters using specified tones.

Modeling the Activity

Place your transparency of the *Tone It Up* handout on the overhead projector. Ask a student to read your letter aloud. Then, ask students to guess the tone of the letter. What wording or parts of the letter led students to make the guesses they made? Discuss how details can help build the tone of a piece of writing.

Activity in Practice

1. Divide the class into teams of three students.

2. Give each team a copy of the *Tone It Up* handout.

3. Using the strips of paper from the *Tone It Up Cutouts* page, give each team a different character's name and a tone.

4. Instruct students on each team to work together to write a letter to their character using the specified tone. Have them discuss reasons why they would be using that particular tone. For example, if the assignment is to write an angry letter to Spider-Man®, students might write one protesting the fact that the superhero left webbing all over their yards. Encourage students to be imaginative and to think about what words they will use to convey that tone.

5. Have the teams write their letters on the handouts. Review the parts of a letter if necessary.

6. After students have completed their letters, have them trade letters with other teams.

7. Ask each team to identify the tone used in the other team's letter. Discuss how the tone affects the information conveyed.

8. Answer and discuss any questions students may have about tone.

Extensions

To modify the activity, have students write letters to the same characters or people but using different tones. Ask the class to compare and contrast their letters.

To extend the activity, have students discuss how tone is important in everyday interactions and different kinds of communication, including E-mail messages and conversations.

Character Mingle and Mix

1. What is the title of your book or story?_____

2. What is the author's name? _____

3. What is your character's name? _____

4. How would you describe your character? _____

   _____

   _____

5. What does your character want? _____

   _____

   _____

6. What conflicts does your character experience?_____

   _____

   _____

   _____

7. What is your character's point of view?_____

   _____

   _____

8. How does your character change throughout the story?_____

   _____

   _____

9. How would your character react to meeting someone new?_____

   _____

   _____

   _____

Plot, Plot, Plot

Event 1 ——— Event 2 ——— Event 3 ——— Event 4 ——— Event 5 ——— Event 6 ——— Event 7 ——— Event 8

1. What is the main conflict or problem? _____

2. How is the conflict or problem finally resolved? _____

3. How is this reading selection organized? Discuss with your team members and write your answer here. _____

What Does It All Mean?

Word	Connotations	Other Meanings

1. What is the overall mood of the passage? _____

2. How do the words above contribute to the mood?_____

   _____

   _____

3. How do these words contribute to the author's style?_____

   _____

   _____

Word Hunt

Root Word, Prefix, or Suffix	Word	What Does the Word Mean?

What Lies Ahead?

1. What is the title of your book or story? _____

2. What is the author's name? _____

3. What was the foreshadowing event? _____

    _____

4. What do you think is going to happen next? Look into the crystal ball and write your
    prediction on the lines below.

5. Why do you think this will happen? Support your prediction with clues from the story
    and your own experiences.

    _____

    _____

    _____

    _____

    _____

    _____

    _____

    _____

Fact Finders

List four facts and one opinion from the ad, article, or flyer you read.

FACT: _____

_____

FACT: _____

_____

FACT: _____

_____

FACT: _____

_____

OPINION: _____

_____

What is the author's purpose? _____

_____

_____

How It Looks to Me

1. What is the title of your book or story? _____

2. What is the author's name? _____

3. What is your character's name? _____

4. What is going on in this scene? _____

    _____

5. How is your character feeling at this moment? _____

    _____

6. What does your character want? _____

    _____

7. What would your character say right now? _____

    _____

Sketch the scene from your character's point of view.

Dark and Stormy Night

Part 1. Think about the key elements of the original story and answer the questions below.

What is the title of the story? _____

How would you describe the setting? _____

How would you describe the mood? _____

How does the story's setting contribute to the mood and plot? _____

_____

_____

Part 2. Change the setting and rewrite the story. If you need more space, continue your story on another sheet of paper or on the back of this sheet.

_____

_____

_____

_____

_____

_____

_____

_____

_____

_____

_____

_____

Theme Team

Theme	Title of Story, Poem, or Play

Which themes appear in more than one work? _____

_____

_____

_____

_____

Mainly So

Write the main idea in the center of the web. Write the supporting details in the other ovals.

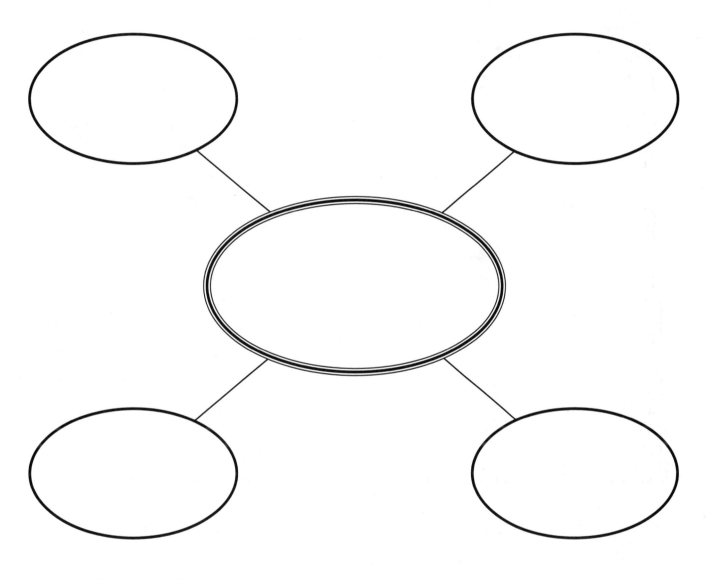

How would you describe the author's purpose? _____

_____

_____

_____

_____

Tone It Up Cutouts

Use the characters and tones listed below for the activity. If desired, add other characters and tones in the empty boxes. Cut out the paper strips along the dashed lines. Store the strips in separate envelopes, one marked "Characters" and one marked "Tones."

Characters	Tones
Snow White	angry
Little Red Riding Hood	happy
Prince Charming	bitter
Frankenstein	sentimental
	sad
	weary
	excited

Tone It Up

(School address) _____

_____

_____

(Date) _____

_____ (Character's name)

_____ (Character's address)

_____

_____

Dear _____,

Hello. We are students in _____ sixth-grade class.

We are writing to you because_____

_____

_____

_____

_____

Sincerely,

_____

_____

_____

(Your names)

Practice Reading Test—Grade 6

Name: _____

Date: _____ Class: _____

Directions: This test contains 4 reading selections and 35 questions. Read each selection. Then, answer the questions. Record your answers on your answer sheet. Be sure to fill in each bubble completely and erase any stray marks. Use the lines provided on the answer sheet to write each short-answer response. If you do not understand a question, ask your teacher for help.

Sample   What is the BEST synonym for the word **exhausted**?

     A   refreshed

     B   ripped

     C   vacuumed

     D   tired   **Sample**   Ⓐ Ⓑ Ⓒ **Ⓓ**

Note to Teacher: This chapter contains a reproducible practice test based on the most common reading standards tested nationwide at the sixth-grade level. This practice test can be given to your students before, during, or after they have completed the activities in Chapter 5. (For a short diagnostic test, see Chapter 3.)

Practice Reading Test—Grade 6

Directions: Read the article. Then, answer questions 1 through 6 on your answer sheet.

Pavlov's Dogs

(1) Ivan Pavlov was a Russian scientist who studied the digestive system. He was interested in the relationship between salivation and the stomach. In a famous experiment, he put bits of meat on dogs' tongues. He then observed their salivation and digestion. Pavlov found out that salivating was a reflex triggered by the sight or smell of food. He also learned that salivation sends a message to the stomach to begin digesting.

(2) Pavlov wondered if other factors could affect the salivation reflex. To find out, he followed the same routine each time he gave the dogs food. He rang a bell just before feeding the dogs. He did this many, many times. Then, after a while, he tried ringing the bell but did not give the dogs food. They salivated anyway. The dogs had learned to associate the bell with food. Pavlov called the dogs' salivation at the sound of the bell a "conditioned response."

(3) Pavlov's experiment showed that all animals can learn, or be conditioned, to behave in certain ways. Pavlov's discovery also helps explain a lot of human behavior. For example, if you get very sick to your stomach after eating some kind of food, the very sight or smell of that food can make you queasy in the future. This queasiness is a conditioned response. We also use the expression "Pavlov's dog" to describe someone who associates a reward with a certain activity. Say, for example, you always go out for ice cream after a visit to the dentist. If the sight of the dentist's chair has your stomach rumbling for ice cream, you are a lot like one of Pavlov's dogs!

GO ON

1 The purpose of the passage is to—

   A question Pavlov's discovery.

   B explain the importance of Pavlov's experiment with dogs.

   C provide a biography of Ivan Pavlov.

   D inform the reader about different dog-training methods.

2 Which of these words has the closest meaning to the word **conditioned**?

   F smoothed

   G strange

   H learned

   J rearranged

3 Which of these people would most likely be compared to Pavlov's dogs?

   A a boy who dreads riding the bus to school

   B someone whose mouth waters before eating

   C a girl who gets thirsty when she hears her sister open a can of soda

   D someone who jumps when the phone rings

4 Why did Pavlov ring a bell before giving the dogs food?

   F to see if the dogs would associate the sound with food

   G because he fed them at one o'clock each day

   H to make sure the dogs were awake

   J to let the dogs know it was okay to begin eating

5 What did Pavlov learn about the role of salivation in digestion?

   A It has no physical function.

   B It is the first step of digestion.

   C It is the final step of digestion.

   D It happens during the entire digestion process.

6 Complete the analogy.

   Mouth is to salivation as _____ is to digestion.

   F dog

   G food

   H stomach

   J tongue

Practice Reading Test—Grade 6 (continued)

Directions: Read the article. Then, answer questions 7 through 12 on your answer sheet.

The Kawésqar

(1)   At the southernmost tip of South America, the land breaks up into many small islands. This area is called Tierra del Fuego, which means "Land of Fire." But despite its name, this part of the world is not very hot. It is cold and rainy because it is so far from the equator.

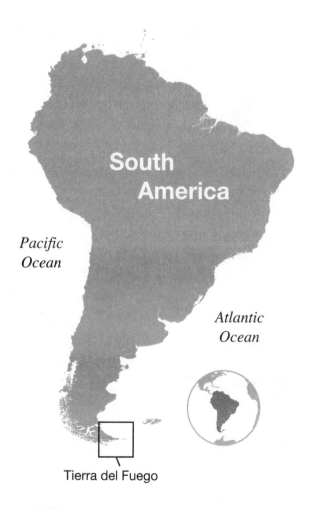

Pacific Ocean

Atlantic Ocean

Tierra del Fuego

(2)   Tierra del Fuego is home to many Native American groups, including the Kawésqar. Because of the cold, the Kawésqar people traditionally kept small fires burning at all times. They were skilled at keeping the fires alive, even in the rain. They traveled among the islands by canoe to fish, building small fires on piles of sand in the middles of their canoes. The first Spanish explorers to see the islands were amazed to see all of the fires and so called the place Tierra del Fuego.

(3)   At the time the Spanish first saw them, there were several thousand Kawésqar living in the area. They lived in oval-shaped huts made of curved branches and sea lion hides. Their diets included seals, fish, and sometimes whales. The father of a Kawésqar family would stand at the front of a canoe with a spear to hunt seals and fish. The women dove for mollusks and other shellfish. The Kawésqar used animal skins to make their clothing.

(4)   Today, the Kawésqar population is very small. Only a handful of people still speak the Kawésqar language, and most of them are quite old. Most of the remaining Kawésqar people live in wood houses on an island called Puerto Edén in the Tierra del Fuego region of Chile. They continue to fish and weave traditional baskets. But the fires of the Kawésqar that gave the region its name no longer burn.

GO ON ▷

7 Which of these was NOT an aspect of traditional Kawésqar culture?

   A horse riding

   B building fires to keep warm

   C basket weaving

   D seal hunting

8 According to the description in paragraph 3, which of the following statements about mollusks is most likely to be true?

   F They swim fast.

   G They are difficult to trap.

   H They don't make good food.

   J They are similar to oysters and clams.

9 What language would the Kawésqar people who don't speak Kawésqar be most likely to speak?

   A Chinese

   B Spanish

   C Sioux

   D English

10 Which of the following is NOT true of the people who speak the Kawésqar language now?

   F They live in South America.

   G Many of them are old.

   H They are no longer nomads.

   J There are hundreds of them.

11 What word BEST describes the tone at the end of paragraph 4?

   A angry

   B sad

   C excited

   D threatening

12 SHORT ANSWER: Answer the following question on your answer sheet. Use complete sentences.

Compare and contrast Kawésqar culture now to the traditional Kawésqar culture described in the passage.

Directions: Read the article. Then, answer questions 13 through 24 on your answer sheet.

The Great Barrier Reef

Notes about the reading

(1)   The Great Barrier Reef is one of the wonders of the natural world. Stretching from Papua New Guinea to the eastern coast of Australia, it is the biggest coral reef ecosystem on the planet. Its unique features support many forms of life that are not found anywhere else.

Reef Facts and Figures

(2)   The Great Barrier Reef is so big that it can be seen by astronauts orbiting the planet. In fact, it is the only living thing on Earth that can be seen from outer space! Basking in the clear, warm waters of the Coral Sea in the southern Pacific Ocean, it is over 1,250 miles (2,000 kilometers) long.

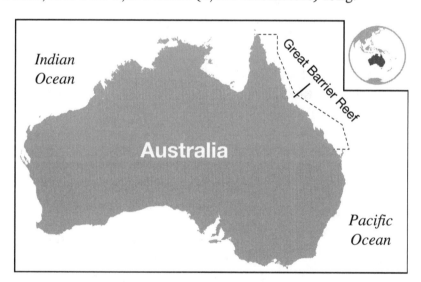

(3)   Although it is called the Great Barrier Reef, the name is a bit misleading. The Great Barrier Reef is not actually a single reef at all. It consists of approximately 2,900 small reefs. These little reefs lie right next to each other. The Reef also contains over 900 islands. It is called a barrier reef because it is an outer reef, separated from the land by a deep, wide lagoon. Another type of reef, called a fringing reef, usually lies closer to the coastlines of mainland and islands.

How a Coral Reef Forms

(4)   Like other reefs, the Great Barrier Reef is made of the bodies of living and dead corals. A coral is a tiny marine polyp, or soft-bodied, **invertebrate** animal that has no backbone. A coral has a cylindrical body. It attaches to rocks at one end and eats with its mouth from the other end. A coral's mouth contains tentacles, and it mostly eats algae.

(5)   There are hundreds of different kinds of coral polyps, each forming variously shaped corals. Reefs can appear bushy, table-like, branching, or even boulder-shaped. Living polyps give coral reefs their bright, beautiful colors. The hard, white part of a reef is made from the skeletons of millions and millions of polyps that have died over thousands of years.

(6)   Most reefs form on hard surfaces in the ocean, such as along the edges of rocky islands. In addition to the dead corals, sand, rubble, and other organisms **accumulate** to build reefs gradually. Reefs grow slowly at a rate of just one centimeter (under half an inch) per year. Since it is made up of so many different reefs, the actual age of the Great Barrier Reef is difficult to determine. The foundations of the Reef may be millions of years old while the living sections are still relatively young.

Unique Marine Life

(7)   The Great Barrier Reef supports a great variety of plant and animal life. Some of these creatures do not exist anywhere else on Earth. Over 1,500 types of fish and hundreds of different corals and birds live in the Great Barrier Reef. The Reef is also home to 4,000 species of mollusks, 500 species of seaweed, 16 species of sea snakes, and 6 species of marine turtles.

Notes about the reading

Practice Reading Test—Grade 6 (continued)

(8) These distinctive creatures attract thousands of visitors each year. Many of the Reef's fish and corals are brilliantly colored, drawing curious scuba divers and snorkelers from all over the world. Imagine swimming with bright pink fish or staring at a sea snake! Some visitors choose to fly over the Reef in airplanes or helicopters. Others like to stay on the land and watch the birds or hike through the rain forest that is part of the Great Barrier Reef's ecosystem. Tourist visits to the Reef bring in more than one billion Australian dollars each year.

A Protected Site

(9) In 1981, the World Heritage Trust listed the Great Barrier Reef as a rare, protected site. The listing recognizes the Reef as a place of unusual beauty and cultural value. The listing also helps maintain the Reef's amazing marine life. Part of the Reef was also established as the Great Barrier Reef Marine Park, further protecting that part of the reef.

(10) However, some people are concerned about the damage to the Reef. Some tourists are not careful and have harmed the Reef by walking on it, dropping anchors and scuba gear on it, or breaking off pieces of coral to take home. Pollution to the ocean and overfishing of the area have also caused damage to the Reef's unique marine life. Conservationists are trying to get more of the Reef recognized as a protected area. Visitors are encouraged to be mindful while exploring the Reef so that future generations can enjoy its amazing charms.

Notes about the reading

13   What is the main idea of the article?

    F   The Great Barrier Reef lies off the coast of Australia.

    G   Some parts of the Great Barrier Reef are protected as a marine park.

    H   The Great Barrier Reef is relatively young compared to other reefs.

    J   The Great Barrier Reef is an important natural formation.

14   Why is the name of the Great Barrier Reef not completely accurate?

    A   It is quite small in size.

    B   It is not a single reef.

    C   It does not form a barrier.

    D   It is composed of living corals.

15   According to the article, what gives coral its brightly colored appearance?

    F   the warm water around it

    G   sand and broken shells

    H   living coral polyps

    J   the reflection of fish

16   According to the article, what do sea snakes and marine turtles have in common?

    A   Both animals are peaceful but will attack scuba divers when pestered.

    B   Species of both animals live in the Great Barrier Reef.

    C   Both animals lay eggs along rocky islands in the Great Barrier Reef.

    D   Both animals eat mainly algae and polyps.

17   According to paragraph 10, which of the following has probably caused damage to the Great Barrier Reef?

    F   flying over it in airplanes and helicopters

    G   cold water from nearby melting glaciers

    H   oil spills in the surrounding waters

    J   people swimming with and observing turtles

Practice Reading Test—Grade 6 (continued)

18 The diagram below shows ideas presented in the article.

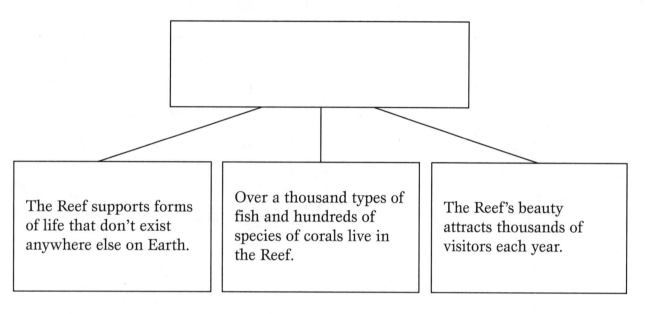

Which main idea belongs in the empty box of the diagram?

A How the Great Barrier Reef is the biggest natural wonder

B Why the Great Barrier Reef is unique and valuable

C How the Great Barrier Reef developed over many years

D Where the Great Barrier Reef lies in the Pacific Ocean

19 In paragraph 6, which phrase helps the reader know what the word **accumulate** means?

F "to build reefs gradually"

G "dead corals, sand, rubble"

H "along the edges"

J "are still relatively young"

20 Which conclusion about coral reefs can the reader draw from the article?

    A They exist mostly in cool, tropical waters.

    B They can be found in the dark, deep sea.

    C They take thousands of years to develop.

    D They have no natural predators except fish.

21 What is the meaning of the word **invertebrate** in paragraph 4?

    F round

    G shiny

    H relaxed

    J spineless

22 According to the article, what makes up most of the hard part of a reef?

    A green algae

    B dead corals

    C pink sand

    D sea worms

23 Which of the following statements is an OPINION in the article?

    F The first coral reefs formed millions of years ago.

    G The Great Barrier Reef is home to thousands of mollusks.

    H The Great Barrier Reef is damaged by people walking on it.

    J The Great Barrier Reef is an amazing natural wonder.

24 Why did the author write this article?

    A to entertain readers with a story about sea animals and plants

    B to persuade readers to join the World Heritage Trust

    C to inform readers about the features of a natural phenomenon

    D to warn readers about the dangers of scuba diving in Australia

Practice Reading Test—Grade 6 (continued)

Directions: Read the story. Then, answer questions 25 through 35 on your answer sheet.

True and Untrue
Adapted from a Norwegian folktale

Notes about the reading

(1) Once upon a time there were two brothers. One was called True and the other Untrue. True was always kind and good to everyone, but Untrue was bad and full of lies. No one ever believed what he said. Their mother was a widow and had very little money. As soon as her sons had grown up, she was forced to send them away so that they might earn their living in the world. She gave each of them a little bag with some food in it. Then, she sent them on their way.

(2) When they had walked until evening, True and Untrue sat down on a log in the wood and took out their bags. They were hungry after walking the whole day and thought a morsel of food would be good.

(3) "I have an idea," said Untrue. "I think we had better eat out of your bag so long as there is anything in it. After that, we can eat from my bag."

(4) True thought that was a great idea, so they started eating from his bag. But Untrue took all of the best bits and stuffed himself with them, while True got only the burnt crusts and scraps.

(5) The next morning, they ate more of True's food. They ate lunch from his bag, too, and then there was nothing left. After they had walked until late at night and were ready to eat once again, True asked to eat out of his brother's bag, but Untrue said, "No, the food is mine. I only have enough for myself."

(6) "But you know you ate out of my bag as long as there was anything in it," said True.

(7) "All very fine," answered Untrue. "If you are such a fool as to let others eat up your food right in front of you, then you must make the best of it, for now all you have to do is sit here and starve."

Notes about the reading

(8)   "Good!" said True. "You're Untrue by name and untamed by experience. So you have been, and so you will be all your life long."

(9)   When Untrue heard this, he flew into a rage and put a curse on his brother. Poor True found that there was a mask over his eyes that he could not remove.

(10)   "Now see if you can tell whether someone is untrue or not!" exclaimed Untrue. And with that, he ran away and left his brother.

(11)   Poor True went walking along, feeling his way through the thick wood. Alone and unable to see, he hardly knew which way to turn but soon caught hold of the trunk of a great bushy oak. He climbed up into the branches and sat there until morning for fear of wild animals.

(12)   "When the birds begin to sing," he said to himself, "I will know that it is day, and I can try to grope my way farther on." After he had sat there a little time, he heard someone come and begin to make a stir and clatter under the tree. Soon after, others came, and when they began to greet each other, he found out it was Bruin the Bear, Slyboots the Fox, and Longears the Hare who had come to gather under the tree. They began to eat, drink, and be merry, and when they were done, they fell to gossiping among themselves.

(13)   Slyboots said, "Let's each tell a little story while we sit here."

(14)   Well, the others had nothing against that. It would be good fun, and so the bear began, for he was king of the company.

(15)   "The King of Ranchland," said Bruin, "has such bad eyesight, he can scarcely see a yard before him. If he only came to this oak in the morning, while the dew is still on the leaves, and took and rubbed his eyes with the dew, he would get back his sight as good as ever."

(16)   "That's all very well," said the fox, "but if the King of Ranchland truly knew, he would not be so badly off for clear water in his own palace. Under the great stone in his palace yard is a spring of the clearest water one could wish for, if he only knew to dig for it there."

(17) "Ah!" said Longears in a small voice. "The King of Ranchland has the finest orchard in the whole land, but it does not bear so much as a nut, for there lies a heavy leaden chain of bad luck in three turns round it. If he got that bad luck up, there would not be another garden like it in all of his kingdom."

(18) "Very true, I dare say," said the fox, "but now it's getting very late. We may as well go home." So, they all went away together.

(19) After they were gone, True fell asleep as he sat up in the tree. When the birds began to sing at dawn, he woke up, took the dew from the leaves, and rubbed it on his face where the mask was. Lo and behold, the mask disappeared, and he could see more clearly than ever before.

(20) True went straight to the King of Ranchland's palace next and got to work at once. He saw the king come out into the palace yard. The king wanted to drink out of his pump, for the day was hot. But when they poured him out a glass, it was muddy and nasty, and the king became quite **vexed**.

(21) "I don't think there is anyone who has such bad water in his yard as I!" cried out the king.

(22) "Well, you have said enough, your Majesty," glittered True. "If you would let me have some men to help me, you would soon see lots of good water coming up."

(23) The king agreed and before he knew it, a jet of water sprang out high up, clear and full. This was very good.

(24) The next day, the king was out in his palace yard again. True overheard the king say, "How I wish there was someone who could tell me a cure for my eyes. I wish to see my garden and the trees."

(25) "I can tell you," said True, remembering the oak. Then, he told the king, who set off at once to find the oak. His eyes were quite cured by the oak dew, and from that time forth, there was no one the king held so dear as True.

Notes about the reading

Notes about the reading

(26) One day, as they were walking together in the orchard, the king said, "I can't tell how it is. There isn't a man in Ranchland who spends as much time on his orchard as I, and yet I can't get one of the trees to bear so much as a pear."

(27) "Well, well!" said True. "If I may have what lies three times twisted round your orchard and men to dig it up, your orchard will bear plenty."

(28) The king was quite willing to part with his chain of bad luck, so True got men and began to dig. All at once, the king's orchard sprang to life, bearing so much fruit that the boughs of the trees hung down, laden with sweet apples and pears nobody had ever seen before.

(29) The king was so happy, he made True his royal advisor and ordered a celebration. At the festivities, in came a beggar so ragged and wretched that everyone sighed. It was True's brother, Untrue.

(30) "Do you know you have seen me before?" said True. "Untrue by name and untrue by nature, my next of kin shall have some mercy food. After that, if you hear anything that can do you good, you will be lucky."

(31) Untrue did not wait around to listen. He got the whole story from people at the party. "If True has gotten so much," he muttered to himself, "what good may I get?"

(32) Later, he climbed up into the oak tree. All of the beasts came as before, ate and drank, and gathered under the tree. When they had finished eating, Slyboots the Fox wished that they should begin to tell stories, and Untrue got ready to listen with all of his might. But Bruin the Bear was in a bad mood.

(33) Bruin growled and said, "Somebody has been chattering about what we said last year, so now we will hold our tongues." And with that, the beasts bade one another good night and left, leaving Untrue just as unwise as he had been before.

25 Which of the following is a theme in the story?

   F It pays to be honest and kind to others.

   G People should remember their origins.

   H Planning ahead makes things easier.

   J Slow and steady wins the race.

26 How do True and Untrue's attitudes differ at the beginning of the story?

   A True knows where they are going, but Untrue is confused.

   B True worries about animals, but Untrue is fearless.

   C True is willing to share, but Untrue is greedy and dishonest.

   D True looks forward to adventure, but Untrue is nervous.

27 "True and Untrue" is an example of—

   F a poem.

   G an epic.

   H an essay.

   J a fable.

28 Why does True climb into the oak tree?

   A He does not like sleeping on the wet ground.

   B He is afraid of being attacked by wild animals.

   C He wants to get a good view of the forest.

   D He needs to look out for Untrue's reappearance.

29 Which word BEST describes True after he arrives at the king's palace?

   F embarrassed

   G grateful

   H helpful

   J hungry

30 What does the word **vexed** mean in paragraph 20?

   A amused

   B lively

   C annoyed

   D animated

Practice Reading Test—Grade 6 (continued)

31 What is the BEST evidence that True is a good brother to Untrue?

    F He listens carefully to what the animals have to say.

    G He gives Untrue food after Untrue shows up at the palace.

    H He tells Untrue how he acquired his knowledge and luck.

    J He invites Untrue to live with him as an advisor to the king.

32 What would be a good title for the story if it were retold from the king's point of view?

    A "How My Kingdom Was Improved"

    B "Last Chance to Defeat the Knights"

    C "How Untrue Served My Foes"

    D "The Oak Tree and the Animals"

33 The words **untrue** and **unwise** share a common—

    F suffix.

    G prefix.

    H root word.

    J definition.

34 Which statement describes a FACT from the story?

    A The King of Ranchland is a kind man.

    B True is a better person than Untrue.

    C True and Untrue are brothers.

    D Slyboots, Bruin, and Longears spot Untrue sitting in the oak tree.

35 SHORT ANSWER: Answer the following question on your answer sheet. Use complete sentences.

How do the characters True and Untrue live up to their names in the story? Support your answer with details from the text.

END OF PRACTICE TEST

Practice Reading Test—Grade 6
Answer Sheet

Directions: Mark your answers on this answer sheet. Be sure to fill in each bubble completely and erase any stray marks. Use the lines provided to write each short-answer response.

1 (A) (B) (C) (D)

2 (F) (G) (H) (J)

3 (A) (B) (C) (D)

4 (F) (G) (H) (J)

5 (A) (B) (C) (D)

6 (F) (G) (H) (J)

7 (A) (B) (C) (D)

8 (F) (G) (H) (J)

9 (A) (B) (C) (D)

10 (F) (G) (H) (J)

11 (A) (B) (C) (D)

12 SHORT ANSWER: Use the space below to answer the question in complete sentences.

Compare and contrast Kawésqar culture now to the traditional Kawésqar culture described in the passage.

_____

_____

_____

_____

_____

_____

_____

_____

_____

_____

_____

13 (F) (G) (H) (J)

14 (A) (B) (C) (D)

15 (F) (G) (H) (J)

16 (A) (B) (C) (D)

17 (F) (G) (H) (J)

Practice Reading Test—Grade 6 (continued)

Answer Sheet

18 Ⓐ Ⓑ Ⓒ Ⓓ

19 Ⓕ Ⓖ Ⓗ Ⓙ

20 Ⓐ Ⓑ Ⓒ Ⓓ

21 Ⓕ Ⓖ Ⓗ Ⓙ

22 Ⓐ Ⓑ Ⓒ Ⓓ

23 Ⓕ Ⓖ Ⓗ Ⓙ

24 Ⓐ Ⓑ Ⓒ Ⓓ

25 Ⓕ Ⓖ Ⓗ Ⓙ

26 Ⓐ Ⓑ Ⓒ Ⓓ

27 Ⓕ Ⓖ Ⓗ Ⓙ

28 Ⓐ Ⓑ Ⓒ Ⓓ

29 Ⓕ Ⓖ Ⓗ Ⓙ

30 Ⓐ Ⓑ Ⓒ Ⓓ

31 Ⓕ Ⓖ Ⓗ Ⓙ

32 Ⓐ Ⓑ Ⓒ Ⓓ

33 Ⓕ Ⓖ Ⓗ Ⓙ

34 Ⓐ Ⓑ Ⓒ Ⓓ

35 SHORT ANSWER: Use the space below to answer the question in complete sentences.

How do the characters True and Untrue live up to their names in the story? Support your answer with details from the text.

_____

_____

_____

_____

_____

_____

_____

_____

_____

_____

_____

_____

Skill-Building Math Activities

This chapter includes 11 different activities designed to help you build and reinforce students' mathematical skills. Each activity provides an engaging way for students to practice one or more key skills that will be assessed on your state's standardized tests. Students will be asked to use their knowledge, experiences, and imaginations. Each activity is structured in the following format:

- ✗ Skills/State Standards—breakdown of the skills addressed in the activity
- ✗ Description—brief summary of the activity
- ✗ Materials You Need—list of materials required for the activity
- ✗ Getting Ready—tips for the teacher and a description of what to do in order to prepare for the activity
- ✗ Introducing the Activity—suggestions for introducing the activity and capturing students' interest
- ✗ Modeling the Activity—ideas for demonstrating the activity (if applicable)
- ✗ Activity in Practice—step-by-step instructions for working through the activity
- ✗ Extensions—variations, extensions, and other teaching suggestions

The activities in this chapter are designed to be hands-on and group-oriented, requiring active participation by your students. However, they are also flexible in nature and can be modified to meet your students' needs, as well as give students individual practice. You can use the activities in any order. You may find that some are more suited to the particular needs of your students than others.

Some activities also include reproducible pages. These pages are found at the end of this chapter, beginning on page 134.

The matrix on pages 110 and 111 organizes the activities by the predominant skills or standards they address. Some activities address more than one skill and may, therefore, appear under more than one category on the chart.

Matrix of Skills Addressed in Math Activities

Skill/State Standard	Activity	Page
Identifying, comparing, and ordering rational numbers	Let's Be Rational ....112 Just Your Average Day 132	
Identifying factors and multiples	Ratio Stars ....120 Flash Math ....124 Pie and Pi 128	
Using fractions, decimals, and percents	Let's Be Rational ....112 Menu Math...............................114 Ratio Stars ....120 What Are the Chances?............122 Pie and Pi 128	
Writing and evaluating algebraic expressions, equations, and function rules	Menu Math...............................114 Making Problems 126	
Applying order of operations	Making Problems 126	
Rounding and estimating	Let's Be Rational ....112 Menu Math...............................114 Flash Math ....124 Making Problems 126	
Using ratios and proportions	Map Happy ....116 Ratio Stars ....120 Pie and Pi 128	
Using tables, symbols, words, and variables to express patterns and relationships	Menu Math...............................114 Map Happy ....116 High Low, High Low ....118 Ratio Stars ....120 What Are the Chances?............122 Making Problems 126	
Geometric measurement	Map Happy ....116 Pie and Pi ....128 What's Your Point? 130	
Graphing points on coordinate planes	What's Your Point? 130	

Matrix of Skills [continued]

Skill/State Standard	Activity	Page
Using mean, median, mode, and range	Just Your Average Day 132	
Measuring time and temperature	High Low, High Low 118	
Measuring weight and capacity	Pie and Pi 128	
Converting units	High Low, High Low ....118 Pie and Pi 128	
Identifying, making, and comparing graphs	Map Happy ....116 High Low, High Low ....118 Ratio Stars ....120 Just Your Average Day 132	
Understanding probability	What Are the Chances?............122 Making Problems 126	
Using problem-solving strategies	Map Happy ....116 What Are the Chances?............122 Making Problems 126	
Collecting, organizing, displaying, and interpreting data	Map Happy ....116 High Low, High Low ....118 Ratio Stars ....120 Just Your Average Day 132	
Applying math to real-world situations	Menu Math................................114 Map Happy ....116 High Low, High Low ....118 Ratio Stars ....120 Making Problems ....126 Pie and Pi ....128 Just Your Average Day 132	

Let's Be Rational

Description

In this competitive game activity, each student will be given a slip of paper and asked to write an integer, fraction, decimal, or mixed number between -3 and 3. You will collect the slips of paper, shuffle them, and ask each student to pick a number. Students will then work in teams to put their numbers in order from least to greatest and record their numbers on number lines. They will also round each number to the nearest place. The team that completes their handout first—and correctly—wins the activity. Students will also check each other's work by exchanging handouts with other teams.

> ### Skills/State Standards
> X Identifying, comparing, and ordering rational numbers
> X Using fractions, decimals, and percents
> X Rounding and estimating

Materials You Need

- *Let's Be Rational* reproducible (page 134)
- Blank slips of paper
- Small prize for winning team (optional)
- Overhead projector and supplies

Getting Ready

Make student handouts using the *Let's Be Rational* reproducible. Make an additional copy on a transparency to use during the modeling portion of the activity.

Introducing the Activity

Review whole numbers, integers, fractions, mixed numbers, and decimals with students. Tell students that they must understand how to compare and order rational numbers, including fractions and decimals. As a warm-up exercise, you may want to write the following numbers on the board and have the class compare and order them:

$$0.15 \qquad 1\tfrac{1}{5} \qquad -5 \qquad 0.005 \qquad \tfrac{5}{2} \qquad 15$$

Answer any questions students have about comparing and ordering rational numbers, and tell students that they will be practicing those skills in this activity.

Modeling the Activity

Using your transparency of the *Let's Be Rational* reproducible, model how to complete the handout using the six numbers given at the bottom of page 112.

Activity in Practice

1. Pass out blank slips of paper to the class. Ask each student to think of a number between -3 and 3 and to write the number on the piece of paper. Remind students that the numbers can be whole numbers, integers, fractions, mixed numbers, or decimals.
2. Collect the numbers, shuffle them, and redistribute them to students.
3. Divide the class into teams of five or six students. Ideally, each team will have the same number of students.
4. Give each team a copy of the *Let's Be Rational* handout. Ask students to look over the handout, and then answer any questions they may have about rounding or using number lines.
5. Tell students that they will compete to complete their handouts as quickly as possible. The team that completes their handout first—and correctly—wins.
6. Keep track of the order in which the teams finish their handouts. After all of the teams are done, discuss their results. Have teams trade handouts to check each other's results.
7. If desired, award the winning team with a small prize.
8. Answer any questions students may have about comparing and ordering rational numbers, rounding, and using number lines.

Extensions

You can modify the activity by making it noncompetitive. If you do this, give students as much time as they need to compare and order their numbers. You can also change the range of numbers students choose from, having them compare only positive numbers, for example.

Extend the activity by asking students to write all of the team members' numbers as fractions or decimals.

Menu Math

Description

In this activity, students will use menus from local restaurants to answer mathematical questions. Taking information from the menus, they will work in teams to add, subtract, multiply, and divide decimals; calculate percents in the form of tax and tips; and write equations to solve word problems. This activity will give students practice with the real-world situation of calculating amounts in restaurants.

Materials You Need

- *Menu Math* reproducible (page 135)
- Menus from several restaurants
- Overhead projector and supplies

Skills/State Standards

- ✗ Using fractions, decimals, and percents
- ✗ Writing and evaluating algebraic expressions, equations, and function rules
- ✗ Using tables, symbols, words, and variables to express patterns and relationships
- ✗ Rounding and estimating
- ✗ Applying math to real-world situations

Getting Ready

Collect at least six menus from local restaurants. (You will want a different menu for each team of students.) Many restaurants offer paper menus you can take with you, while others list their menus on-line or in your local phone book.

Select an additional menu to use during the modeling portion of the activity. Copy this menu onto a transparency.

Make student handouts using the *Menu Math* reproducible. Make an additional copy on a transparency and use it to model the activity.

Introducing the Activity

Review currency amounts and the use of decimals with students. Tell them that when they make purchases, they will often have to add, subtract, multiply, and divide decimals. This is especially true when eating in a restaurant with a large group of people. Explain that in this activity students will practice making the same calculations they would make if they were figuring out a bill in a restaurant.

Modeling the Activity

Display your sample menu on the overhead projector. Choose several menu items to order. Then, write those items and their costs on your transparency of the *Menu Math* handout. Complete the handout, answering students' questions as you go.

Activity in Practice

1. Divide the class into teams of three to five students. Distribute copies of the *Menu Math* handout.

2. Give each team a menu. Have students on each team look over the menu and decide what they want to order. Instruct them to list each item and its cost in the chart on the handout.

3. Then, have each team calculate the total cost of their items. Review addition of monetary values if necessary.

4. Have students calculate tax and tips. Review percents if necessary. Have each team add the total, tax, and tip to get the real amount they would pay for their bill.

5. Have students write an equation for calculating how to split the bill evenly among members of the team. Remind them to use a different variable for each part of the equation: total, tax, tip, and each student's share. Although any variables will do, you might want to instruct students to use the following:

   T = total
   X = tax
   P = tip
   A = how much each student owes

6. After students complete the handouts, discuss their results. Answer any questions they may have about the activity.

Extensions

You can modify the activity by using different imaginary items. For example, you could bring in a variety of catalogs and have students select items to buy from those catalogs. If you do this, have students calculate shipping costs instead of tips.

You can also have students work within a specified budget. Assign them an amount, such as $30, and instruct them to choose their items within this budget. You may want to ask students to round amounts to figure out if they have enough money to order their items, and then adjust their orders if necessary.

You can extend the activity by asking students to calculate what each of them would pay if they did NOT split the bill evenly. Each student would determine her own individual total, then calculate tax and tip based on that total. For an additional challenge, you can have the student make a circle graph of what she spent out of the total bill.

Map Happy

Description

In this activity, students will look at maps and identify the different types of angles they see (acute, right, obtuse, and straight). They will record this information in tables and then use the data to answer questions about ratios of one type of angle to another. They will also use the data to graph their findings. At the end of the activity, students will decide which strategies to apply to find actual distances on the map and to measure the angles they identified.

Materials You Need

- City street maps
- *Sample Map* reproducible (page 136)
- *Map Happy* reproducible (page 137)
- Overhead projector and supplies

Skills/State Standards

- ✗ Geometric measurement
- ✗ Using tables, symbols, words, and variables to express patterns and relationships
- ✗ Using ratios and proportions
- ✗ Using problem-solving strategies
- ✗ Identifying, making, and comparing graphs
- ✗ Collecting, organizing, displaying, and interpreting data
- ✗ Applying math to real-world situations

Getting Ready

Select one or more city street maps to use for this activity. Each map should include a scale and show streets that clearly form angles at intersections. Consider using maps of local areas to engage students' interest. You may also want to consider copying and enlarging just a small portion of a map, showing 15 to 30 different angles.

Create a transparency of the *Sample Map* reproducible to use during the modeling portion of the activity.

Make student handouts using the *Map Happy* reproducible. Make an additional copy on a transparency and use it to model the activity.

Introducing the Activity

Review basic map-reading skills with students. Also, review the different types of angles (acute, right, obtuse, and straight) and how to measure them, ratios, and various kinds of graphs. Explain to students that they will practice taking geometric measurements, calculating ratios, and making graphs in this activity.

Modeling the Activity

1. To model the activity, display your *Sample Map* transparency on the overhead projector. Mark all of the angles formed by the intersections of streets. Then, ask students to identify each type of angle.

2. Show students the *Map Happy* transparency and complete the table showing the number of each type of angle.

3. Calculate the ratios of different types of angles.

4. Make a graph of your results. Explain why you chose that particular type of graph.

Activity in Practice

1. Divide the class into teams of three to five students.

2. Give each team a map and a *Map Happy* handout.

3. Instruct each team to use the map to complete the handout. Answer any questions students may have about angles, ratios, graphs, and map scales. If necessary, help them decide what kinds of graphs to use to display their results and help them make the graphs.

4. After students complete their handouts, discuss their results. Have teams trade handouts to review each other's work. Answer any questions they may have about the activity.

Extensions

The first time students try this activity, you can modify it by leaving out certain steps on the handout if you think they are too challenging. For example, you might want to leave the graphing section for another time.

If you have trouble finding appropriate maps for this activity, use the *Sample Map* handout or create your own map.

To extend the activity, have students identify geometric shapes they see in the map and then measure the angles they identify.

High Low, High Low

Description

In this activity, students will work in teams to collect data about high and low temperatures in different cities around the world, including their own city or town. Students will convert the temperatures between degrees Fahrenheit and Celsius. Each team will then decide which kind of graph to use to best display the data students have gathered. At the conclusion of the activity, teams will compare their completed graphs and answer questions using the data shown on the graphs.

Materials You Need

- *High Low, High Low* reproducible (page 138)
- Weather sections of newspapers
- Graphing paper and rulers
- Internet access (optional)

Skills/State Standards

- ✗ Measuring time and temperature
- ✗ Identifying, making, and comparing graphs
- ✗ Collecting, organizing, displaying, and interpreting data
- ✗ Using tables, symbols, words, and variables to express patterns and relationships
- ✗ Converting units
- ✗ Applying math to real-world situations

Getting Ready

Make sure students have access to global weather information for this activity. Bring in copies of your local newspaper and/or other papers with national distribution. Alternatively, arrange for students to use the Internet to find the weather data they need.

Make student handouts using the *High Low, High Low* reproducible.

Introducing the Activity

Review how to measure temperature with students, making sure they know how to read a thermometer. Show students how to find weather information in a newspaper or on-line. Tell students that in this activity they will be gathering weather information in order to make graphs. You may also want to review the different types of graphs with students.

Activity in Practice

1. Divide the class into teams of four students. Give the teams graphing paper and rulers to make their graphs.

2. Distribute copies of the *High Low, High Low* handout.

3. Instruct teams to find the high and low temperatures for each city in the table for one particular day and record their results. Convert temperatures between Fahrenheit and Celsius. Review the conversion formulas below if necessary:

$$F = \tfrac{9}{5}C + 32 \qquad\qquad C = \frac{5(F-32)}{9}$$

4. Then, have each team decide which type of graph would be best to represent the data they have gathered. You may need to review the purposes of different types of graphs in order to help them decide. Students should realize that bar graphs are the best choice.

5. Instruct students to make their graphs using the graphing paper and rulers. Ask teams to present their results and explain their graph choices.

6. Have students answer the questions that follow the table on the handout.

7. Answer any questions students may have about graphing, measuring temperature, and converting units.

Extensions

To extend the activity, you can have each group record temperatures in the cities over a week or more and then graph the results. If you do this, ask students how the type of graph they use might differ. (Students should realize that a line graph is the best choice to display results over an extended period of time.)

To modify the activity, supply students with the data they need or complete the table for them and have them focus just on graphing skills. You could also tell them which kind of graph to use, although comparing graphs is an important skill for them to learn.

You could also add other cities to the table. Incorporate cities that students are currently studying in their social studies classes.

Ratio Stars

Description

In this activity, students will determine ratios of students with certain characteristics to those with differing characteristics (such as long hair to short hair) within their teams. They will represent these ratios as pictures, in words, and as fractions and percentages. They will also reduce the ratios to lowest terms whenever possible. Then, students will work with proportions to calculate how many members of the team would have a particular characteristic if one of the numbers in the ratio was multiplied by another number.

Materials You Need

- *Ratio Stars* reproducible (page 139)
- Overhead projector and supplies

Skills/State Standards

- ✗ Using ratios and proportions
- ✗ Using fractions, decimals, and percents
- ✗ Identifying factors and multiples
- ✗ Identifying, making, and comparing graphs
- ✗ Using tables, symbols, words, and variables to express patterns and relationships
- ✗ Collecting, organizing, displaying, and interpreting data
- ✗ Applying math to real-world situations

Getting Ready

Make student handouts using the *Ratio Stars* reproducible. Make an additional copy on a transparency to use during the modeling portion of the activity.

Introducing the Activity

Review ratios and proportions with students. Remind students that ratios can be written in several different ways. To demonstrate this, tell students that your desk drawer contains two pens for every three pencils. The ratio of pens to pencils is 2 to 3 and can be written in any of the following formats:

$$2:3 \qquad ^2/_3 \qquad 0.67 \qquad 67\%$$

Explain to students that equal ratios are proportions. Example: $^2/_3 = {}^4/_6$

Tell students that in this activity they will be working with ratios based on a variety of characteristics of students in their class.

Modeling the Activity

Ask students to help you determine the ratio of students wearing athletic shoes to students wearing other types of shoes. Then, using your transparency of the *Ratio Stars* handout, demonstrate how to use this ratio to find the proportions asked for in Part 2.

Activity in Practice

1. Divide the class into teams of six to eight students. Give each team a copy of the *Ratio Stars* handout.

2. Have students on each team determine the ratios asked for in Part 1 of the handout. Tell them to draw the ratios first, then describe them in words, and finally write them as fractions and percentages. (Students may need to use the backs of the handouts or additional paper.)

3. Have students reduce the ratios to lowest terms. Review how to do this if necessary.

4. Then, have students work with proportions to answer the questions in Part 2. You may want to have students modify the numbers in Part 2 so that they are even multiples of the numbers in the ratios from Part 1. Help each team modify their numbers before they proceed.

5. Ask the teams to present their results. Answer any questions students may have about the activity.

Extensions

You can extend the activity by having students make circle graphs of the different ratios.

To modify the activity, have students work together as a class (rather than in teams) to answer the questions about ratios. Alternatively, you could reduce the number of different ratios each team is working with.

What Are the Chances?

Description

In this activity, students will work in teams to determine the probability of various events occurring. Given bags of multicolored marbles, gum balls, or other similar objects, students will make diagrams, tables, or pictures to show all of the possible color combinations they could draw if they were to pick three items at random. This activity will give students the opportunity to practice probability while also using their problem-solving skills.

Skills/State Standards

X Understanding probability

X Using fractions, decimals, and percents

X Using tables, symbols, words, and variables to express patterns and relationships

X Using problem-solving strategies

Materials You Need

- *What Are the Chances?* reproducible (page 140)
- Marbles, gum balls, or similar multicolored objects
- Small cloth or paper bags
- Crayons or colored pencils

Getting Ready

Assemble small bags of marbles, gum balls, or other multicolored objects. Each bag should contain five to eight objects in a variety of colors, including blue and red. Make one bag for each team of students.

Make student handouts using the *What Are the Chances?* reproducible.

Introducing the Activity

Review the concept of probability with students. Tell them that probability is the likelihood that something will occur. Remind students that probability can be described in whole numbers and words, as in "She has a 1 in 5 chance of making that shot," or in percentages, as in "She has a 20% chance of making that shot." Ask students to brainstorm examples of real-life situations in which probability is used. Weather reports and sports predictions are just two examples.

Activity in Practice

1. Divide the class into teams of three to five students.

2. Give each team a bag of marbles (or gum balls or other objects), crayons or colored pencils, and a copy of the *What Are the Chances?* handout.

3. Instruct students to empty their bags and count each type of marble. Have them record the numbers on their handouts.

4. Have each team make a diagram, table, or picture to show every color combination possible if three marbles are picked randomly from the bag. Encourage students to choose the method of representation they feel most comfortable with and answer any questions they have about making diagrams or tables.

5. Next, instruct teams to answer the questions on their handouts. Have them write their answers as whole numbers (1 in 5) and as percentages (20%).

6. Ask each team to present their diagrams, tables, or pictures and to discuss their findings.

7. Answer any questions students may have about the activity.

Extension

To extend the activity, have teams draw three marbles from their bags 10 separate times and record the results. Discuss how their actual results compared with the probability diagrams or tables they made.

Flash Math

Description

In this competitive game activity, student teams will race against each other to identify factors, multiples, or estimated sums. Using an overhead projector or index cards, you will "flash" pairs of numbers and ask the teams to find each pair's greatest common factor, least common denominator or multiple, or estimated sum. The team that gets the most correct answers wins.

Skills/State Standards

X Identifying factors and multiples

X Rounding and estimating

Materials You Need

- Overhead projector and supplies (or index cards)
- Scratch paper

Getting Ready

There is no handout for this activity. To prepare, you will need to generate 30 or more number pairs. If an overhead projector and supplies are readily available, write down each number pair on a separate transparency. If an overhead projector is not available, use index cards to make flash cards of number pairs.

When selecting number pairs, keep in mind the specific skills you want students to practice. For example, if you want them to practice finding greatest common factors, be sure the numbers in each pair have factors in common. Once you have chosen the number pairs, keep the answers readily available.

Introducing the Activity

Discuss factors and multiples with the class. Tell them that identifying greatest common factors, least common denominators or multiples, and estimated sums are skills that they will be tested on. Explain that in this activity they will compete to find greatest common factors, least common denominators or multiples, and/or estimated sums for different pairs of numbers.

Modeling the Activity

Demonstrate the activity with a simple pair of numbers. Write the numbers 6 and 15 on the board or on an overhead transparency. Ask students to identify the greatest common factor (3), least common multiple (30), and then estimated sum (20). Explain to students that they will perform these same sorts of calculations in this activity. Answer any questions that students may have.

Activity in Practice

1. Divide the class into four or five teams.

2. Give each team sheets of scratch paper to use when making calculations.

3. Decide what you want students to practice identifying first. For example, you may want to have students identify least common multiples first. Tell students what they will be identifying for each number pair.

4. Explain to students that you will flash a series of number pairs on the projector screen (or using flash cards). The goal is to be the first team to identify the least common multiple (or greatest common factor or estimated sum) for each pair. The first team that gets the correct answer scores one point. The team that scores the most points wins.

5. Flash each pair of numbers and keep track of the scores on the board.

6. After you have gone through all of the number pairs, determine a winner. Present the winning team with a small prize if desired.

7. Discuss factors, multiples, and estimating sums with students. Answer any questions they may have about the activity.

Extension

Extend the activity by having students write prime factorizations for each number flashed. Review how to write prime factorizations with exponents if necessary.

Making Problems

Description

In this activity, students will work in teams to determine the best ways to solve different types of word problems. Solving these problems will require students to use a variety of skills, including making lists and tables, identifying patterns, translating words into pictures, writing equations, and using logical reasoning.

Materials You Need

- *Making Problems* reproducible (page 141)
- Scratch paper
- Overhead projector and supplies

Getting Ready

Make a transparency outlining some important problem-solving steps.

Skills/State Standards

- ✗ Using problem-solving strategies
- ✗ Writing and evaluating algebraic expressions, equations, and function rules
- ✗ Applying order of operations
- ✗ Using tables, symbols, words, and variables to express patterns and relationships
- ✗ Rounding and estimating
- ✗ Understanding probability
- ✗ Applying math to real-world situations

1) Read the problem carefully.
2) Underline important information in the problem. Circle what you need to find or solve for.
3) Choose a strategy (such as making a chart or drawing a picture) and discuss steps to solve the problem.
4) If appropriate, estimate an answer to the problem.
5) Make an equation or expression to help you solve the problem.
6) Work the steps to solve the problem.
7) Check your answer.

Next, prepare a sample word problem to share with students during the modeling portion of the activity. Write out the problem on a transparency. Use the following problem or create one of your own.

> Shirley and Curtis have 49 books together. They gave 1 book to their friend Eliot. Then, they divided their book collection into 2 equal parts. How many books does Shirley have now?

Finally, make student handouts using the *Making Problems* reproducible.

Introducing the Activity

Tell students that in this activity they will work together in teams to solve a variety of word problems. Using the transparency you created during the "Getting Ready" section, discuss the steps they might take when approaching a word problem. Review any other problem-solving strategies students may need to know.

Modeling the Activity

1. Show students the transparency you made of the sample word problem. Ask a student volunteer to read the problem aloud.

2. Model how to solve the problem by underlining important information and circling what is to be found. Then, write an equation to help solve the problem. Using the sample problem given on page 126, the equation would look like this:

$$\text{Number of books } X = (49 - 1) / 2$$
$$X = 24 \text{ books}$$

3. Discuss order of operations in solving equations and answer any questions students may have about how you approached and solved the problem.

Activity in Practice

1. Divide the class into teams of three to five students.

2. Distribute scratch paper and copies of the *Making Problems* handout.

3. Ask students to solve the problems, helping them with any steps they find troublesome. Remind teams to discuss how they will solve each problem before tackling it.

4. Problem 3 requires students to write an equation. Make sure that students do this correctly and review the order of operations with them.

5. Discuss how rounding and estimating can be useful in problem solving. Ask students to determine when it makes sense to guess an answer.

6. Discuss team results and answer any questions students may have about problem solving.

Extensions

To extend the activity, have each team create three or four word problems for another team to solve. Encourage students to think of a variety of types of problems. Have teams trade problems and solve them.

To give students additional practice with probability, ask them to determine the chances of Alex being first in line in Problem 2 of the handout.

Pie and Pi

Description

In this activity, students will use a simple recipe as the basis for practicing a variety of math skills. Working in teams, students will measure ingredients for a pie filling, perform operations with fractions, convert fractions to percents, use ratios and proportions, find the circumference of a circle, and convert measurements from customary to metric. This activity will also give students the opportunity to practice math skills in a way they might use in a common, real-world situation.

Materials You Need

- *Pie and Pi* reproducible (page 142)
- Kitchen scale
- Measuring cups and spoons (customary and metric, if available)
- Recipe ingredients (See *Pie and Pi* reproducible)
- Access to a kitchen and necessary baking tools (optional)
- Overhead projector and supplies (optional)

<table>
<tr><td colspan="2">Skills/State Standards</td></tr>
<tr><td>X</td><td>Measuring weight and capacity</td></tr>
<tr><td>X</td><td>Using fractions, decimals, and percents</td></tr>
<tr><td>X</td><td>Identifying factors and multiples</td></tr>
<tr><td>X</td><td>Using ratios and proportions</td></tr>
<tr><td>X</td><td>Geometric measurement</td></tr>
<tr><td>X</td><td>Converting units</td></tr>
<tr><td>X</td><td>Applying math to real-world situations</td></tr>
</table>

Getting Ready

Investigate whether you and your students can have access to the school kitchen for this activity. If so, plan to perform the activity in the kitchen. If not, bring in the recipe ingredients along with a kitchen scale and various measuring cups and spoons, and perform the activity in your classroom. *Note: Before completing any food activity, ask parental permission and inquire about students' food allergies. Common food allergies include peanuts and other nuts, dairy, eggs, and berries. Also, parents may have religious or other preferences that will prevent some students from eating certain foods.*

Make student handouts using the *Pie and Pi* reproducible. You may also wish to create a transparency or handout for student reference that lists several common measurement conversions. Here are a few conversions you might want to include:

1 teaspoon = $\frac{1}{6}$ ounce	1 teaspoon = 5 milliliters
1 tablespoon = $\frac{1}{2}$ ounce	1 tablespoon = 15 milliliters
1 cup = 8 ounces	1 cup = 237 milliliters
1 pint = 2 cups	1 pint (liquid) = 473 milliliters
1 quart = 2 pints	1 ounce = 28 grams
1 gallon = 4 quarts	1 pound = 0.454 kilograms

Introducing the Activity

Tell students that in this activity they will be working with a recipe for pie filling. They will be asked to make various calculations using the recipe.

Activity in Practice

1. Divide the class into teams of four students.

2. Distribute copies of the *Pie and Pi* handout.

3. Instruct students to read the ingredients and their amounts. Answer any questions they have about weight and capacity measurements. At this point, you may want to ask students how to convert these units within the customary system. (For example, ask how many cups are in a pint.)

4. Have teams work together to answer the questions that follow the recipe on the handout.

5. Ask students to measure out the recipe ingredients. If you have metric measuring tools available, instruct students to check their conversions as well.

6. Answer any questions students may have about fractions, multiplication, ratios, formulas for a circle, and conversions between customary and metric units.

Extensions

If you have access to the school kitchen, you could have students actually make the pie filling and pies. (The filling mixture can be poured into a frozen crust and baked according to directions on package.) Alternatively, students can make these measurements at home as part of their homework, then bake the pies and bring them to school.

Any recipe can be substituted in the handout to give students more practice with measurement and other skills.

What's Your Point?

Description

In this activity, student teams will use blank graphs to create geometric figures with five vertices. After they have drawn their figures, teams will trade papers with each other. Each team will then work to identify the coordinates of every vertex in the figure the other team drew. When they have identified all five vertices, students will pass those coordinates on to a third team to see if that team can replicate the original drawing on a piece of graph paper using only the given coordinates. This simple but fun activity works along the same lines as a game of Telephone or Operator, in that information is susceptible to change as it is passed on from one team to the next. It gives students meaningful practice graphing points on coordinate planes and can also be extended to have them determine perimeter and area.

> ### Skills/State Standards
> ✗ Graphing points on coordinate planes
> ✗ Geometric measurement

Materials You Need
- *What's Your Point?* reproducible (page 143)
- Graph paper
- Overhead projector and supplies

Getting Ready

Each team of students will need two or more sheets of graph paper in order to complete the activity. Every student will also need one sheet of graph paper to use during the modeling portion of the activity.

Take one sheet of graph paper and photocopy it onto a transparency. Draw a sample figure on the transparency that contains four vertices. Label the coordinates of each vertex. Save this transparency to use to model the activity.

Make student handouts using the *What's Your Point?* reproducible.

Introducing the Activity

Review geometric shapes, angles, and vertices with students if necessary. Then, discuss the use of a coordinate grid, including the position of the x-axis and y-axis, as well as the correct way to write a coordinate pair. Tell students that they will be making geometric figures and identifying coordinates in this activity.

Modeling the Activity

Give each student a sheet of graph paper. Then, using the sample figure you drew, call out the coordinates of the four vertices. Have students write down these coordinates, then attempt to draw the prescribed figure. When the students are done, show them the transparency with your original figure. How many of the students' drawings match your own? Explain to students that they will be following a similar procedure in this activity.

Activity in Practice

1. Divide the class into teams of three to five students.

2. Distribute graph paper and a copy of the *What's Your Point?* handout.

3. Instruct students on each team to work together to draw a figure with five vertices. The figure can be any shape, but the vertices should lie on precise coordinates in the plane.

4. When they are finished drawing their figures, have teams trade handouts with each other.

5. Ask each team to identify the coordinates of the five vertices in the shape the other team has drawn. Have them record those coordinates on the handout, then write them again at the top of a clean piece of graph paper to pass on to a third team.

6. Have the third team plot the given coordinates in an attempt to recreate the original shape made by the first team.

7. Have teams compare their results. Were they able to replicate the shapes accurately?

8. Discuss the students' results. Then, answer any questions they may have about coordinates and graphing.

Extensions

You can vary the activity by having students draw shapes with more or fewer vertices.

You can extend the activity by having students find the area of each shape. They could also measure the perimeter with a ruler.

Just Your Average Day

Description

In this activity, students will use their birthdays as the basis for exploring mean, median, mode, and range. Working in teams, students will first generate a list of numbers based on the day of the month each of them was born. Then, they will make various calculations using those numbers. Finally, teams will discuss the significance of finding different types of averages, as well as the advantages and disadvantages of each.

Materials You Need

- *Just Your Average Day* reproducible (page 144)
- Sample pool of seven or eight numbers (test scores, teacher ages, etc.)
- Overhead projector and supplies (optional)

Skills/State Standards

X Using mean, median, mode, and range

X Identifying, comparing, and ordering rational numbers

X Applying math to real-world situations

X Collecting, organizing, displaying, and interpreting data

X Identifying, making, and comparing graphs

Getting Ready

Prepare a sample pool of numbers (based on real or fictional data) to use during the modeling portion of the activity. For example, you could compile a short list of seven test scores or the ages of seven different teachers. Once you have chosen your numbers, write them down.

Make student handouts using the *Just Your Average Day* reproducible.

Introducing the Activity

Review how to find each type of average: mean, median, and mode. Then, ask students to brainstorm situations in which they might use these different averages in real life. Tell students that they will be working with mean, median, mode, and range in this activity.

Modeling the Activity

List your sample pool of numbers on the board or on a transparency. Ask students to help you find the mean, median, mode, and range of the numbers. Talk students through each step, showing your work on the board. Alternatively, have students talk *you* through each step. Discuss any questions students may have.

Activity in Practice

1. Divide the class into three teams.

2. Distribute copies of the *Just Your Average Day* handout.

3. Instruct students on each team to survey their team members and record all of their birth dates on the handout.

4. Have students work together to calculate mean, median, mode, and range based on their teams' numbers. These numbers should be recorded on the handout.

5. When they are done with their calculations, ask students which type of average is most useful in this situation. Have them determine what each average tells them about the team.

6. Answer any questions students may have about averages.

Extensions

You can modify the activity by having students find the averages for other sets of data, such as height or length of hair.

To extend the activity, have students graph their results, choosing an appropriate type of graph to best display the information.

Let's Be Rational

> List your team members' numbers on the lines below.
>
> _____ _____ _____
>
> _____ _____ _____

1. List the numbers again, this time in order from least to greatest.

   _____

   _____

2. Mark the numbers on the number line.

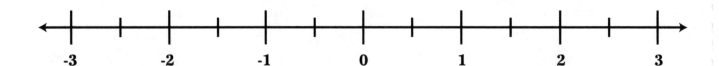

3. Using the number line, round each number to the nearest one.

   _____ _____ _____

   _____ _____ _____

4. Which number is closest to zero? _____

Menu Math

Look at the menu. Decide what each team member wants to order and write the items in the chart below.

Student's Name	Food and Drink Items Ordered	Cost

1. What is the total cost of your order? _____

2. Calculate the tax on your total.
   Use a tax rate of 8%. _____

3. Add the tax and the total. _____

4. Now, calculate the tip. A tip is
   usually 15% of the total before tax. _____

5. Add the total, tax, and tip. (This is the amount
   you would actually pay in a restaurant.) _____

6. Imagine that you are splitting the cost of the bill
   evenly with the rest of your team. Write an equation
   for calculating how much each person owes. _____

   Provide a key that shows what each variable
   stands for. _____

7. Using your equation, calculate how much each
   member of the team would pay. _____

Sample Map

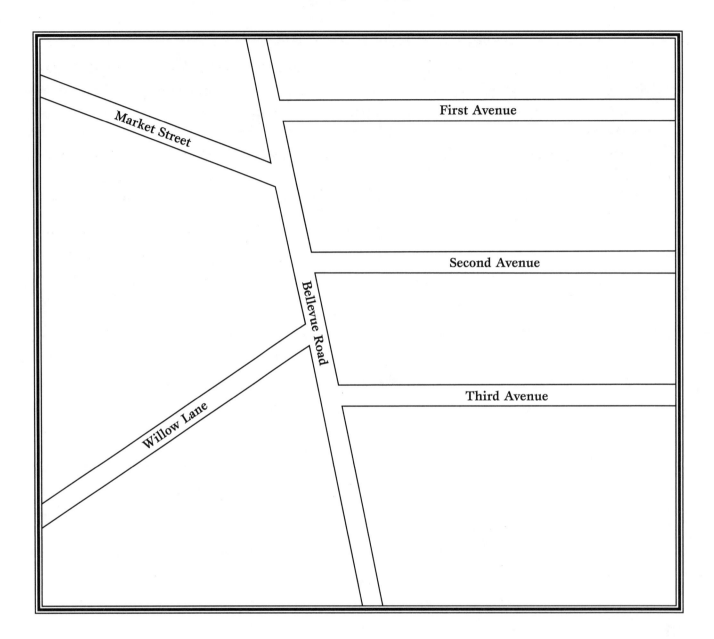

First Avenue

Market Street

Second Avenue

Bellevue Road

Third Avenue

Willow Lane

0   1   2   3

1 inch = 1 mile

Map Happy

Look at your map. Identify the following angles. Write how many of each type of angle you see:

Type of Angle	Acute	Right	Obtuse	Straight
Number of Angles in Map				

1. What is the ratio of acute angles to straight angles on your map? _____

2. What is the ratio of obtuse angles to right angles on your map? _____

3. In the space below, make a graph that shows the different types of angles on your map.

4. Look at the scale on your map. Describe in words a strategy you can use to find the actual distance between points on your map.

_____

_____

5. Describe how you can measure the angles you identified.

_____

_____

High Low, High Low

Find the day's high and low temperatures in degrees Fahrenheit or Celsius for each of the following cities. Record the temperatures in the table.

City	High Temperature °F	°C	Low Temperature °F	°C
Your town:				
Austin, Texas				
New York, New York				
San Francisco, California				
New Orleans, Louisiana				
Tampa, Florida				
Chicago, Illinois				
Budapest, Hungary				
Copenhagen, Denmark				
Seoul, South Korea				
Jakarta, Indonesia				
Cairo, Egypt				
Cape Town, South Africa				
Lima, Peru				
Rio de Janeiro, Brazil				

Convert the temperatures you found to Celsius or Fahrenheit. Record them in the table above. On another sheet of paper, graph the data you have gathered. Then, answer the questions.

1. Which city had the highest temperature ? _____

2. Which city had the lowest temperature? _____

3. Why did you choose the type of graph you used? _____

4. What other types of graphs could you have used? _____

_____

Ratio Stars

Part 1. Based on the members of your team, determine the ratios listed below. Write each ratio as a sentence and draw a picture to represent it. Then, show the ratio as a fraction and as a percentage. Reduce each ratio to lowest terms.

1. girls to boys: _____

   _____

   _____

2. brown eyes to green eyes: _____

   _____

   _____

3. long hair to short hair: _____

   _____

   _____

4. glasses to no glasses: _____

   _____

   _____

5. blue shirts to red shirts: _____

   _____

   _____

Part 2. Use proportions to answer the questions.

6. If there were 10 girls in your group, how many boys would there be? _____

7. If 12 people had green eyes, how many would have brown eyes? _____

8. If 30 people had long hair, how many would have short hair? _____

9. If 60 people wore glasses, how many people would have no glasses? _____

10. If 1,000 people were wearing blue shirts, how many would be wearing red shirts? _____

What Are the Chances?

Complete the table by writing how many objects there are of each color in the bag.

Blue	Red	Green	Yellow	_____

In the space below, make a diagram, table, or drawing to show every color combination that is possible if three objects are drawn from the bag.

1. What are the chances that a blue object will be picked if one object is drawn? _____

2. What are the chances that a red object will be picked if two objects are drawn? _____

Making Problems

Solve the problems in the space provided. Circle your answers.

1. Annie's library book was 5 days overdue. The fine she had to pay was 10¢ for the first day, 25¢ for the second day, and $1.00 for every day after that. How much money does Annie owe?

2. Alex, Bob, Moses, and Chris were standing in line to get into the zoo. How many different ways can they order themselves in line?

3. Ole bought 2 shirts that were originally priced at $33.50 each. Each shirt was on sale for $3.50 off the original price when Ole bought them. What is the total sale price of the 2 shirts?

4. Naima asked Nayan to guess her favorite number in 10 questions or less. It took Nayan 6 tries to guess Naima's favorite number. What questions do you think Nayan asked?

Pie and Pi

Read the ingredients for a pie filling.

3 pounds peaches or plums
¼ cup flour
1 tablespoon lemon juice
½ teaspoon ground cinnamon
¼ teaspoon salt
honey

Makes filling for one 8-inch pie.

Use the ingredients list to answer the questions.

1. What is the ratio of cinnamon to salt in this recipe?   _____

2. If you used 1 teaspoon of cinnamon,
   how much salt would you use?   _____

3. If you tripled the recipe to make filling for 3 pies,
   how much flour would you use?   _____

   Write this number as a percent and as a fraction.   _____

4. Imagine that you have baked the pie. The diameter
   of the pie is 8 inches. What is the pie's circumference?   _____

   What is the pie's radius?   _____

5. Convert the measurements to metric units.

   3 lbs. = _____ kg   ½ tsp. = _____ mL

   ¼ c. = _____ mL   ¼ tsp. = _____ mL

   1 Tbsp. = _____ mL   8 in. = _____ cm

What's Your Point?

On the grid below, draw a geometric figure with five vertices.

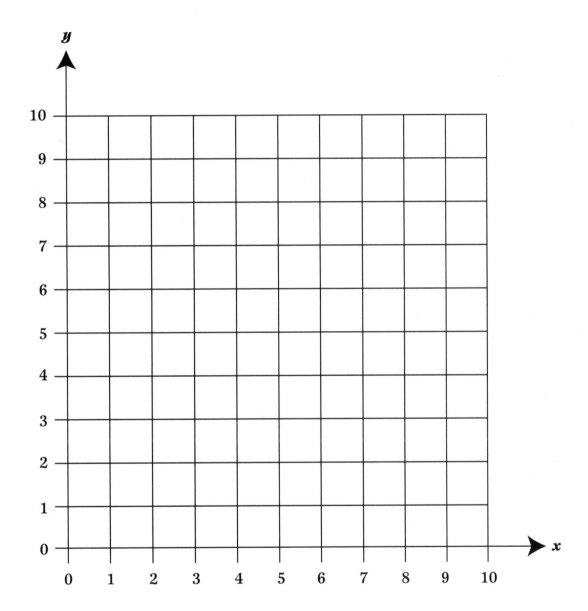

List the coordinates of all five vertices.

_____ _____ _____ _____ _____

Just Your Average Day

1. Write down the day of the month each person on your team was born.

   _____   _____

   _____   _____

   _____   _____

   _____   _____

   _____   _____

2. Calculate the mean for this set of numbers. _____

3. Now, list the numbers in order from least to greatest. Circle the median.

   _____

   _____

4. Is there a mode? If so, write it here. _____

5. What is the range for this set of numbers? _____

6. Which statistic (mean, median, or mode) best describes the numbers in this set? Why?

   _____

   _____

Practice Math Test—Grade 6

Name: _____

Date: _____   Class: _____

Directions: This test contains 38 math problems, a math reference chart, and an answer sheet. Read each problem carefully. Mark your answers on your answer sheet. If you do not understand a question, ask your teacher for help.

Note to Teacher: This chapter contains a reproducible practice test based on the most common math standards tested nationwide at the sixth-grade level. This practice test can be administered to your students before, during, or after they have completed the activities in Chapter 7. (For a short diagnostic test, see Chapter 3.)

Practice Math Test—Grade 6 (continued)

Directions

Read each problem carefully. You will mark most answers on your answer sheet by filling in the correct bubble.

Sample 1 The school bus was $^3/_5$ empty.
What percent of the bus was empty?

  A 40%

  B 75%

  C 25%

  D 60%   **Answer:** Ⓐ Ⓑ Ⓒ ⬤D

For some problems, you will be asked to determine the answer and fill in a bubble grid on your answer sheet. Follow these steps:

1. Work the problem and find an answer.
2. Write your answer in the boxes across the top of the grid.
    - Print only one digit or symbol in each box.
    - Be sure to write a dollar sign, fraction bar, or decimal point in the answer box if it is part of the answer.
3. Fill in the corresponding bubble in each column.
    Do NOT fill in bubbles in the empty columns.

  Sample 2 Mario bought a CD for $13.25, including tax. He paid for the CD with a $20 bill. How much change did Mario receive?

  Answer: $6.75

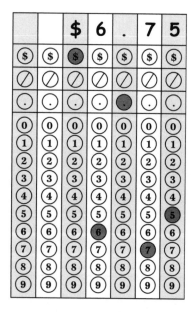

For all other types of problems, follow the directions given on the test page.

Practice Math Test—Grade 6 (continued)

Math Reference Chart — 1

Length

Customary	Metric
1 foot = 12 inches 1 yard = 3 feet 1 mile = 1,760 yards 1 mile = 5,280 feet	1 centimeter = 10 millimeters 1 meter = 100 centimeters 1 kilometer = 1,000 meters

Mass and Weight

Customary	Metric
1 pound = 16 ounces 1 ton = 2,000 pounds	1 gram = 1,000 milligrams 1 kilogram = 1,000 grams

Capacity

Customary	Metric
1 cup = 8 ounces 1 pint = 2 cups 1 quart = 2 pints 1 gallon = 4 quarts	1 centiliter = 10 milliliters 1 deciliter = 10 centiliters 1 liter = 1,000 milliliters

Time

1 minute = 60 seconds 1 hour = 60 minutes 1 day = 24 hours 1 week = 7 days	1 year = 365 days 1 year = 52 weeks 1 year = 12 months

Simple Interest

$I = prt$

I = interest
p = principal
r = rate
t = time

continued on next page

Math Reference Chart — 2

Key

l = length	P = perimeter	A = area
w = width	SA = surface area	V = volume
s = length of a side	d = diameter	B = area of the base of a solid
b = base	r = radius	
h = height	C = circumference	$\pi \approx 3.14$ or $\frac{22}{7}$

The sum of the interior angles of a polygon is equal to $180(n-2)$,
where n is the number of sides in the polygon.

Perimeter

square $\quad P = 4s$
rectangle $\quad P = 2(l+w)$

Circumference

circle $\quad C = 2\pi r$ or πd

Pythagorean Theorem

$a^2 + b^2 = c^2$

Area

□	square	$A = s^2$
▭	rectangle	$A = lw$ or bh
△	triangle	$A = \frac{1}{2}bh$ or $\frac{bh}{2}$
▱	trapezoid	$A = \frac{1}{2}(b_1 + b_2)h$ or $\frac{(b_1 + b_2)h}{2}$
▱	parallelogram	$A = bh$
○	circle	$A = \pi r^2$

Surface Area

	cube	$SA = 6s^2$
	rectangular solid	$SA = 2(lw) + 2(hw) + 2(lh)$
	cylinder (total)	$SA = 2\pi rh + 2\pi r^2$

Volume

	cube	$V = lwh$
	rectangular solid	$V = lwh$
	prism	$V = Bh$
	cylinder	$V = \pi r^2 h$
	pyramid	$V = \frac{1}{3}Bh$

Practice Math Test—Grade 6

1 Mimi's sister is 203 cm tall. What is 203 cm expressed in meters?

A 0.203 m

B 2.03 m

C 20.3 m

D 203 m

2 Amy recorded 5 temperatures for a winter week in her city. Which list shows the temperatures in order from coolest to warmest?

F -14° F, -10° F, 0° F, 3° F, 6° F

G 3° F, 6° F, 0° F, -14° F, -10° F

H -10° F, -14° F, 0° F, 6° F, 3° F

J -14° F, 0° F, -10° F, 3° F, 6° F

3 Susan wants to tile her bathroom using rectangular tiles. Each tile is 3 inches wide and 8 inches long. Susan wants to cut down some of the tiles to 1.5 inches wide. How long should the smaller tiles be in order to stay proportional to the larger ones?

A 3.0 in.

B 3.5 in.

C 4.0 in.

D 4.5 in.

3 in. / 8 in.

4 Which value of x will make the equation below true?

$$3^x = 81$$

F 1

G 2

H 3

J 4

5 The table shows Russell's age compared to his mother's age at different times.

Russell's Age	Russell's Mother's Age
3	33
5	35
10	40
12	42
14	44

Let r represent Russell's age and m represent his mother's age. Which equation shows the relationship between their ages?

A $r = m + 30$

B $m = r - 32$

C $r = m - 32$

D $m = r + 30$

GO ON

6 The graph below shows the number of sixth-grade students who played in the marching band for Travis Middle School over a 5-year span.

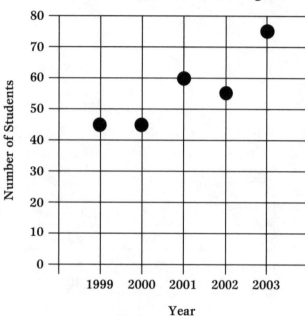

Sixth-Grade Students in the Travis Middle School Marching Band

Which is the best estimate of the total number of students playing in the marching band from 1999 to 2003?

F 120

G 190

H 240

J 280

7 A box is shaped like a cube with an edge that is 6 feet long. What is the volume of the box?

A 36 ft.^{3}

B 216 ft.^{3}

C 225 ft.^{3}

D 1,296 ft.^{3}

8 Ava built a fence around her dog Parker's doghouse to keep him from running away. The length of different parts of the fence are shown in the diagram below.

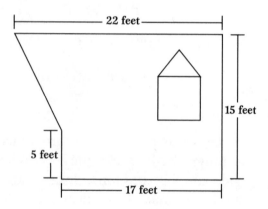

What is the total area enclosed by the fence?

F 330 ft.^{2}

G 255 ft.^{2}

H 280 ft.^{2}

J 305 ft.^{2}

GO ON ➡

Practice Math Test—Grade 6 (continued)

9 The circumference of a circle is 19 inches. Find the approximate length of the circle's radius.

A 3 in.

B 4 in.

C 5 in.

D 6 in.

10 By 4:00 P.M., 75% of the girls on the soccer team at Sun Valley High School had completed their warm-up exercises at practice. What fraction of the team had NOT yet finished their warm-up exercises?

Record your answer in the bubble grid below and on your answer sheet. Write your answer across the top and fill in the corresponding bubbles in each column.

11 Under certain conditions, 0.4 inches of rain is equal to 8 inches of snow. Which fraction best represents this ratio of rain to snow?

F $^{20}/_1$

G $^{20}/_4$

H $^1/_{20}$

J $^8/_{0.4}$

12 At a pizza party, each pizza was cut into 8 equal-sized slices. Lalo ate $3^1/_2$ slices, Danielle ate 4, Sebastian ate 3, and Eliana ate $2^1/_2$. Which expression can be used to find the total slices eaten?

A $^7/_2 + 4 + 3 + ^5/_2$

B $3^1/_2 + 2^1/_2 - (4 + 3)$

C $^7/_8 + ^4/_8 + ^3/_8 + ^2/_8$

D $3 \times 4 + ^7/_2 + ^5/_2$

13 If Liam correctly marked 0.15, $^5/_2$, -0.025, and -$^1/_5$ on a number line, which number would be closest to zero?

$$\xleftarrow{\hspace{0.3cm}}\underset{-6\ -5\ -4\ -3\ -2\ -1\ \ 0\ \ 1\ \ 2\ \ 3\ \ 4\ \ 5\ \ 6}{+\ +\ +\ +\ +\ +\ +\ +\ +\ +\ +\ +\ +}\xrightarrow{\hspace{0.3cm}}$$

F 0.15

G $^5/_2$

H -0.025

J -$^1/_5$

GO ON

14 Look at the map of a neighborhood.

Look at Angle A, formed by the intersection of Nova Street and Harbor Avenue. What type of angle does it appear to be?

A acute

B right

C obtuse

D straight

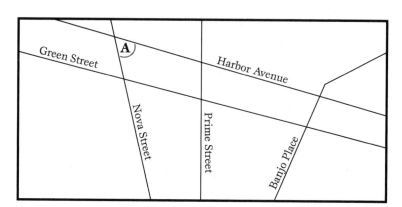

15 The side lengths and perimeters of some regular polygons are shown in the table below.

Regular Polygons

Side Length (cm)	Perimeter (cm)
3	24
4	32
5	40
6	48
7	56

Which geometric figure is represented by the information in the table?

F pentagon

G square

H hexagon

J octagon

16 Junot must buy paper plates and plastic spoons for a picnic. Plates are sold in packages of 10 and spoons are sold in packages of 12. What is the least number of packages of plates and spoons that Junot can buy to have an equal number of plates and spoons?

A 2 packages of plates and 3 packages of spoons

B 4 packages of plates and 5 packages of spoons

C 5 packages of plates and 4 packages of spoons

D 6 packages of plates and 5 packages of spoons